Sales Scripting Mastery

The 7-Step System for Consistently Delivering Successful Sales Presentations

Eric Lofholm

Foreword by Tom Hopkins

ERIC LOFHOLM INTERNATIONAL

Foreword by Tom Hopkins
Editorial direction by Roy Rasmussen
Interior design and layout by Marian Hartsough

Disclaimer: This book is intended to provide information only, and should not be construed as professional sales or business advice. No income claims are stated or implied. How you put this information to use is up to you.

ISBN-10: 0-9898942-1-5
ISBN-13: 978-0-9898942-1-0

Printed in the United States of America

Eric Lofholm
Eric Lofholm International
5701 Lonetree Blvd. Suite 121
Rocklin, CA 95765 United States
(916) 626-6820

Contents

Dedication

*To the millions of people out there whose income
is directly tied to their ability to persuade others.*

Foreword by Tom Hopkins

One of the fastest ways to success is to find someone who is already successful; study what they do; then you do it, too. The hard part for most people is the "you do it, too" part, because whatever those actions are, they're probably outside their current comfort zone. And we humans fight stepping outside our comfort zones both consciously and subconsciously with super human strength.

In my career as a sales trainer, I always teach the exact scripts that worked for me in my own record-setting sales career. I tell my students to first memorize and use the scripts, and then, after they start earning greater incomes, to study the psychology behind the scripts. Once the psychology is understood, most sales pros can write their own scripts, using the words they're most comfortable with.

When you can write your own strategically successful scripts, you can also write your own paycheck—in nearly any amount you want.

In this book, Eric Lofholm breaks down the emotions you'll feel as you consider the value of scripts. He'll help you develop a new mindset about scripts and teach you how to write your own! Eric is a student of words and the psychology of sales. He has combined those two special areas of knowledge into this instruction book to help you develop a sales script that builds from warming up potential clients all the way to closing sales. And he does it in a specific order with each step building on the previous one. It's not overly complicated, but it is a system that needs to be applied in a certain way in order for you to gain the greatest benefit.

If selling is your career, or even if it's just a seasonal job, you'll be saying a lot of the same things over and over again as you work with different clients, right? So, why not say what you're saying in the best possible way—to generate the most sales possible?

When you have that slap-your-forehead moment when you think of what you should have said instead of what you did say, that's you evaluating and re-scripting yourself. When you analyze what you're saying and find ways to make it better, you are scripting your presentations. You're already doing this. Now it's time to start doing it more effectively.

Don't just read through this book. Treat it like the textbook it is. Study it. Make notes about the ideas you discover between these pages. Test the strategies you learn. Then come back to the book again and again to fine-tune your scripts. It's a process, but 100% worth the effort.

You won't regret it.

— Tom Hopkins,
Author of *How to Master the Art of Selling*
and *When Buyers Say No*

Acknowledgments

I would like to acknowledge and thank all those who have influenced my understanding of sales and persuasion, including especially my mentors Dante Perano, Dr. Donald Moine, Tony Martinez, and Jay Abraham; as well as Tony Robbins, Michael Gerber, and Ted Thomas.

Most of all I would like to thank my mother and father; and my children Brandon and Sarah, whose love and support has inspired this book.

Introduction

In the original version of the story of Ali Baba, a poor woodcutter becomes rich overnight after he overhears the magic words that open the door to a cave full of gold: "Open Sesame." In another version of the story from a classic Bugs Bunny cartoon, Daffy Duck's sword-wielding friend Hassan experiences some frustration because he can't remember the right words. "Open Sarsaparilla" and "Open Saskatchewan" don't quite do the trick. Only the right words unlock the door to wealth. Ali Baba got the gold because he knew the script.

I didn't have a script when I started selling. I didn't know the magic words. Not knowing what to say nearly cost me my first sales job.

I quickly discovered I was terrible at selling. I was the bottom producer on the team. At the end of my first year, I was put on quota probation. The quota was $10,000 a month in gross sales. I had missed quota two months in a row. I had just gotten married, so not only my job but also my marriage was at risk. My back was against the wall; I *had* to hit quota or lose my job. But I was facing a seemingly insurmountable problem: my job was selling, and I didn't know how to sell. So I did the only thing that I could think to do. I prayed about it.

My prayers were answered when the number one sales mind in the world, Dr. Donald Moine, came into my life and began to mentor and coach me. Dr. Moine is the author of *Unlimited Selling Power*, which *Success* magazine called the best book ever written on the subject of professional selling. I affectionately call Dr. Moine the Obi-Wan Kenobi (Luke Skywalker's mentor in *Star Wars*) of sales training. Dr. Moine took me under his wing and began to mentor and coach me. With Dr. Moine's help, my results increased. In my make-or-break month, I had sales of $10,500, making quota by $500. The following month, I did $51,000 in gross sales! Seven months later, I did $160,000 in gross sales in a single month!

Now, twenty years later, I'm the author of an Amazon bestseller on sales, *The System*, and I'm widely recognized as one of the top sales trainers in the United States and the world. How did I get from being on sales quota probation to being one of the top sales trainers in the world? The answer is the secret Dr. Moine taught me: the "Open Sesame" that opens the door to wealth. In my last book I revealed part of the magic selling formula I learned from Dr. Moine: the secret of sales sequencing. But in one chapter I briefly touched on an even bigger secret, which is what I'm going to reveal in detail in this book.

The secret is sales scripting.

After twenty years of selling, after spending tens of thousands of dollars studying under the best marketing minds in the world, I can tell you that sales scripting is the most profitable idea I have ever learned. Scripting has generated more revenue for me than any other sales technique. I've helped thousands of clients generate hundreds of millions of dollars of revenue by applying what I know about sales scripting. And now, for the price of this book, I'm going to share that invaluable secret with you.

Why Learning Sales Scripting Is So Valuable

Why is knowing sales scripting so valuable? In my experience, scripting is the best way to help you overcome some of the biggest frustrations sales professionals face. It is also the best way to generate revenue consistently. Sales scripting can help you:

- Overcome anxiety stemming from not knowing what to say during a sales presentation
- Build confidence in your ability to speak, close, and handle objections effectively
- Know what to say in any sales situation, whether speaking one-on-one, from the front of the room, over the phone, or over a webinar
- Ensure that your sales presentations always follow a persuasive sequence steering a clear path to a strong close
- Avoid losing sales by delivering a close prematurely before you've laid a foundation with rapport, probing questions, and benefits
- Build trust and rapport quickly and easily

- Hone your probing questions to identify what your prospect really wants and what's going to make them want to buy
- Present your benefits using powerful words that arouse your prospect's desires
- Close smoothly and naturally without anxiety
- Handle objections with the confidence that comes from being prepared and knowing exactly what to say
- Know how to follow up to turn one sales opportunity into multiple opportunities
- Generate referrals on a regular basis
- Get consistent, predictable sales results from following the same successful script over and over

These are some of the benefits I and my students and clients have experienced from applying sales scripting repeatedly over the past twenty years to generate hundreds of millions of dollars in revenue. I invested well over $30,000 with Dr. Moine to learn his sales scripting secrets. Companies have paid me as much as $20,000 to teach their people what you'll learn in this book. What you learn from reading it will pay for the price of the book many times over if you're selling a product like real estate, autos, or insurance where gaining even a small sales edge translates into thousands of dollars in added revenue. To some of you, this book may be worth millions in added revenue over the lifetime of your sales career.

Getting the Most Out of This Book

I suggest you *study* this book rather than simply just read it. Use a notebook to create a Success Journal where you can record the best ideas you learn from this book and how you're applying them. To help you get started, I've included a Success Journal Notes section at the end of this book with blank pages where you can record the best ideas you learn from each chapter and the best ideas you learn from the book as a whole. As you read, identify the ten best ideas you pick up from reading and record them for quick reference at the end of your Success Journal Notes. (And I left extra lines, so don't worry if you want to write more than ten!)

I have read sections of some of my favorite books numerous times. The reason for this is because I get more out of what the author has to share each time I review it. I suggest that you read over and over again the chapters or sections of the sales process where you need the most help.

Whether you are learning sales scripting or any other aspect of sales, I teach that there are three top ways you can elevate your sales results, and to reflect this, I have divided the book into three parts:

> Part I: Inner Game
>
> Part II: Outer Game
>
> Part III: Action

The inner game is the mental side of sales scripting. It is your beliefs, your comfort zone, how you deal with rejection.

The outer game is the tactical side of scripting: what you say, when you say it, how you say it.

The third component is action, which focuses on moving yourself to follow through on practicing your sales scripts and delivering them consistently with enough activity to generate sales.

While each chapter can be read on its own, the book does follow a logical sequence. You can skip to the chapter you need the most help with, or read the book in sequence.

Here are additional thoughts on how to elevate your results from this material:

- Each chapter can be read as a stand-alone chapter.
- Over time, you will want to read the book completely a total of seven times.
- If you are working on referrals, read that chapter once per day for seven days.
- *Believe* that this book will make you money. (In fact, believe that this book will make you more money than any book you have ever read.)
- Mark the best ideas you encounter with a highlighter or jot them down in your journal notes.

- The fair price for the information you will learn from this book is over $30,000. I want you to read the book as if you paid $30,000 for it.

- This book changes people's lives. As you are reading it, think about the people you care about who you will want to give a copy of this book to.

A Final Note

Before we get started let me share with you a powerful metaphor about how to create possible breakthroughs with your selling.

Imagine a circle. Now imagine a small slice of that pie that represents 3% of the circle. The circle is all the knowledge that exists in the world. The 3% pie slice represents things that you know you know. (For example, you know you are reading *The System*. You know you know your phone number.)

Next, imagine a pie slice that is 7% of the circle. The 7% represents things that you know you don't know. (For example, you probably know you don't know how to fly an airplane.)

That leaves the remaining 90% of the pie. This 90% are the things you don't know you don't know. In other words, this is the unknown realm for you. When you move from the you-don't-know-you-don't-know to the known realm, it creates a *breakthrough possibility*. This book is about sharing ideas, strategies, and concepts that will help you create many breakthroughs in your sales results.

Key Points

I want to share a secret with you. Many of the success stories in this book happened because the person created an *intention* to be one of my success stories. I encourage you to create an intention right now to become one of my success stories—a person that I will talk about in one of my future books, future audio programs, or seminars. And if you are willing to create that intention, I want you to write it down in your Success Journal Notes at the end of this book right now. Then send me an email at wins@ericlofholm.com and declare your new intention to be one of my success stories. This may be one of the most important action items for you in the entire book.

Some of you reading this book know me from my seminars. Others are meeting me for the very first time. I want to acknowledge you for being a person of action. Just by reading this book you are declaring your intention to become better at sales and influence. I want to give a special welcome to those readers who are meeting me for the first time. Thank you for having faith that I can help you and for believing it is possible that I can share something with you that can make a difference for you in your life and your sales results.

Let's begin!

To your success,
Eric Lofholm

The Inner Game of Sales Scripting

Sales greatness starts with the mindset that you can become great.
—Eric Lofholm

Part I of this book focuses on the *mindset* you need for successful scripting.

Some people I meet resist the idea of sales scripting. There are several common reasons. The first one is fear of sounding canned, rehearsed, or mechanical. Another common fear stems from not knowing how to write a sales script and having no idea what to say, which can trigger a form of anxiety similar to writer's block. Both of these fears can lead you to avoid sales scripting, keeping you from enjoying the increased success you could potentially achieve.

In the following two chapters I'm going to teach you how to get past these fears so you can feel confident about sales scripting and enjoy the success that comes from mastering this ultimate sales tool. In the next two chapters I'm going to show you:

- How to get past the fear of sounding like you're reading from a canned sales script and feel confident about being prepared

- How to overcome anxiety about writing sales scripts by applying some strategies similar to those professional writers use to overcome writer's block

Reading, studying, and applying these two chapters will help you cultivate the mindset you need to feel prepared and confident when you apply the sales scripting strategies I'll cover in Part II of this book. You'll get the most out of the chapters on sales scripting if you pay close attention to what you learn in the next two chapters.

Chapter 1

Who's Afraid of Scripting? Getting Past Fear of Sounding Scripted

Sales scripting is the most profitable idea I've ever encountered in all my years in sales, but when I introduce it to new audiences, I inevitably meet some resistance from people who are afraid that scripting will make them sound artificial. They worry that if they apply scripting, they'll come across as canned, phony, or fake, and it will hurt their sales presentation.

The reality is that not scripting is what will hurt your presentation. To understand why, let's consider an analogy to acting, where scripting comes from. Every play and every movie starts with a script. The successful delivery of any scene depends on how well the actors and the actresses in the scene perform the lines from the script. If any actor doesn't know their lines, it slows the whole production down.

Even actors who don't rehearse much on set with other actors spend many hours privately memorizing their lines and practicing their script. For instance, recently Daniel Day-Lewis won the Best Actor Award for *Lincoln*, directed by Steven Spielberg. Now Daniel Day-Lewis is known for not rehearsing with the rest of the cast, but that doesn't mean he doesn't practice the script. He was so dedicated to practicing the script of *Lincoln* that he stayed in character for three straight months during filming. Even Steven Spielberg was required to call him "Mr. President" for three months. During that time Daniel Day-Lewis also practiced the script with Sally Field, who was playing Lincoln's wife, by texting her and carrying on conversations as if they were their characters. No wonder he won Best Actor! But do you think he would have won if he didn't know the words to the Gettysburg Address because he didn't practice?

Winning professional athletes also use scripting. I'm from northern California, so I'm a San Francisco 49ers fan. 49ers head coach Bill Walsh introduced the concept of scripting his team's opening plays. He did this to counter the aggressive defensive blitzing style that had been popularized by the Chicago Bears, which at the time was frustrating every other team in the league. Walsh and his quarterback Joe Montana found that by using a script, they could study holes in the defense, enabling them to call better offensive plays and win more consistently. Walsh's scripting formula proved so successful that he won three Super Bowls, and today most pro football teams script their first fifteen offensive plays. The list of coaches trained by Walsh and his staff who have gone on to not only become head coaches but appear in conference championships and Super Bowls is long and impressive: San Francisco coaches George Seifert and Jim Harbaugh, Packers and Seahawks coach Mike Holmgren, Packers coach Mike McCarthy, Broncos coach Mike Shanahan, Panthers and Broncos coach John Fox, Titans coach Jeff Fisher, Ravens coaches Brian Billick and John Harbaugh, Buccaneers coach John Gruden, Eagles coach Andy Reid, and Seahawks coach Pete Carroll, to name a few. Walsh's legacy proves that scripting works.

Scripting works in sales, too. But first you have to get past the fear of sounding scripted. This chapter will help you with that.

Why You Should Embrace Scripting

A first step towards getting past fear of sounding scripted is appreciating the value of scripting. More than two dozen of my mentor Dr. Moine's clients have earned more than $1 million a year by applying scripting. Some of them have made more than $10 to $20 million a year. In my sales career over the past two decades, I've used scripting to generate nearly $500 million revenue for my clients.

Why do scripts work? Simple: human beings respond in predictable ways. Let me give you an example. If you do what a millionaire does, you'll get what a millionaire has. If you invest your money where millionaires currently have their money invested, what will you become? If you were with me here today, you would say, "A millionaire."

Now, I've asked that question to literally thousands of people, and every person—every person—gives the same answer: a millionaire.

Prediction is a form of power—Dr. Moine

In your presentation, wouldn't you like to know what your prospects are going to say before they say it? Well, that is the power of sales scripting.

Because audience reactions to scripts are predictable, you can borrow other people's scripts. I didn't make up from scratch the script I just shared with you about the millionaire. I borrowed it from someone else. You can do the same: borrow other people's scripts.

If you're still not sure about the power of scripting, listen to what Michael Gerber, one of the world's leading experts on teaching business owners how to raise their level of success and the man behind the book *The E-Myth*, has to say about scripting. This is a direct quote from the book:

Things need to be sold and it's usually people who have to sell them. Everyone in business has heard of the old song 80 percent of our sales are produced by 20 percent of our people. Unfortunately few seem to know what the 20 percent are doing that the eighty percent aren't.

The 20 percent use a system, unlike the other 80 percent!

Let's take this a step farther. Sales scripting is part of your selling system, a fully-orchestrated interaction between you and your customer. A selling system follows five primary steps:

1. Step 1: Identification of the specific benchmarks or consumer decision points in your selling process.
2. Step 2: The literal scripting of the words that will get you to each consumer decision point successfully. (Yes, written down, like the script for a play.)
3. Step 3: The creation of various materials to be used with each script.
4. Step 4: The memorization of each benchmarked script.
5. Step 5: The delivery of each script by your sales representatives in identical fashion.

If you put a sales system involving scripting to work in your company, you will see amazing results regardless of what kind of business you're in.

How much can you earn from scripting? To help you connect with the value of scripting, I've designed the following exercise:

Exercise

1. Take out a sheet of paper or open a program like Microsoft Word.

2. Make a list of the scripts you need. Here is a list to use as a template:

   Main presentation
   Appointment setting
   Referrals
   Front of the room
   Conference calls
   Objection handling
   Follow up
   Recruiting
   Voice mail
   Customer service
   Web copy
   Sales letter
   Email

3. Now that you have your list, prioritize it. When I prioritize my scripts, the three criteria I use are: easiest, most urgent and most valuable. Imagine that you now have all of your scripts written. How much extra income do you believe you will earn in the next 12 months? Write down your answer:

   _____

4. Now imagine how much longer you plan on being in business — 5 years, 10 years, 20 years, or longer. How much extra income do you believe you would earn over the rest of your career? Write down that number:

   _____

5. Now I want to give you permission to dream. Imagine the scripts are done and the money is rolling in. How is your life different? Write down your answer:

   _____

YOUR ANSWERS TO THESE QUESTIONS GIVE YOU YOUR REASONS WHY YOU MUST GET YOUR SCRIPTS DONE ASAP. THE ACHIEVEMENT OF YOUR BIGGEST DREAMS MAY BE DIRECTLY TIED TO YOUR ABILITY TO INFLUENCE OTHERS.

You're Already Using a Script, But Is It a Good Script?

At this point you might be saying, "Okay, Eric, I see how scripting can make me more money, but that doesn't really address my concern about sounding artificial. Won't scripting make me sound less natural and hurt my sales delivery?"

Here's the answer to that I tell audiences:

> *The reality is, whether you think you're using scripts or not, you are using scripts.*

Now you might be saying to yourself right now, "Eric, you don't know what you're talking about. I don't use sales scripts." Yes, you do, and I will share with you why shortly. For now, here's an interesting question: Why do people resist scripting? Most people respond by saying they don't want to sound canned, rehearsed, inauthentic, robotic, they don't feel that scripts are flexible, and so on. If that were *my* view of what scripting is, then I wouldn't want to use scripts either.

However, what if that's not what scripting is? What if scripting is something *totally* different? What if scripting made you more powerful, more persuasive, and helped you and your client at the same time? Would you want to learn more about it? Its power? How it can transform you into a persuasion master? If this speaks to you, then you are reading the right material, at the right time.

If scripting isn't canned, or rehearsed, or inauthentic, or robotic, or inflexible, what is it? Here is Dr. Moine's reply:

> **A script is a series of words in sequence that have meaning.**

In other words, a script is the opposite of a random string of words. This is why I say that in reality, we *all* use sales scripts. You're either using a script or you're speaking in random gibberish.

Of course, you don't speak in gibberish. Let me give you an example. Suppose that I asked you to deliver a presentation today, one that you've never delivered before. You would probably get the details from me, then deliver the best presentation possible. The second time you delivered this presentation, you would repeat much of what you said the first time. The *third* time you delivered this presentation, a lot of what you said the first and second times you'd say again. In other words, you would have effectively *drifted* into a script. People think, "Oh, I don't use scripts because I don't want to be scripted!" In reality, however, you *are* scripted; it's just that you drifted into a script.

If you accept the fact that you use scripts, the key question then becomes this: how *effective* are your scripts? You have two choices. You can either continue to wing it, creating your scripts by drifting into them. Or, you can prepare powerful, persuasive scripts that will make you more confident, more consistent, and add more value to your clients, all of which will bring you more business day after day, presentation after presentation, for the rest of your career.

Consider this example: When a world leader like the President or the Pope or a business leader addressing a group of investors makes a speech, do you think that he makes up that speech as he goes along? Or do you think he's using a prepared script? **You see, when everything counts, people use a prepared script.**

Or imagine that you were the owner of an organization that has fifty sales people. Would you want them using *persuasive* scripts, or would you want them making up their presentations on the fly, so to speak? Of course you would want them using persuasive scripts.

Scripts absolutely are flexible. They are powerful. They are prepared. They are persuasive. Simply put, sales scripting is the most *powerful* way for you to improve your presentation results. Wow, pretty important, right? Let me repeat that…seven times:

Sales scripting is the most powerful way for you to improve your presentation results.

Sales scripting is the most powerful way for you to improve your presentation results.

Sales scripting is the most powerful way for you to improve your presentation results.

Sales scripting is the most powerful way for you to improve your presentation results.

Sales scripting is the most powerful way for you to improve your presentation results.

Sales scripting is the most powerful way for you to improve your presentation results.

Sales scripting is the most powerful way for you to improve your presentation results.

Exercise

If you're ready to use sales scripting to make more sales, sign your name here:

❑ **Yes! I plan to use sales scripting in all my presentations and key interactions.**

Signed: _____

Date: _____

Defeat Anxiety with Preparation

Here's another reason to use scripting: scripting is the best way to combat sales anxiety. To understand why, let's imagine two mixed martial arts fighters about to fight their first professional match. The first fighter has been training every day for ten years under top coaches, followed a strict conditioning regimen, practiced their techniques for eight hours a day, and sparred against experienced practice partners for multiple rounds every day. The other fighter skips training sessions, doesn't have a coach, doesn't stick to their conditioning routine, rarely practices their techniques, and has only sparred a few times against weak opponents. Which of the two fighters do you think is going to feel more nervous when it comes time to fight?

Now let's consider how preparation plays a similar role in sales anxiety. Imagine you're an insurance sales representative and you're trying to sell a policy, and your prospect wants to know how your provider's policy compares to that of a rival company. If you don't know the answer because you haven't studied your sales literature, how confident are you going to feel responding to the prospect's question? How do you think that lack of confidence is going to affect your sales presentation? How will it affect your credibility your prospect?

One place preparation plays a major role in determining whether you feel anxious or confident about a sale is in your close. For instance, I and my sales trainers have observed that many public speakers trying to sell from the front of the room do a good job delivering most of their presentation, but when it comes time to ask for a sale they suddenly freeze up and start fumbling for words. Why is that? Part of the answer is often that they haven't practiced a closing script because they're afraid to ask for a sale and they've procrastinated about deciding what they're going to say, and now they're trying to figure out what to say on the spot, and they're terrified that they can't figure out what to say. You don't have to put yourself through this if you practice a closing script.

Objection handling is another place where preparation is crucial to your confidence level. If your prospect responds to your close with a tough objection you've never thought about before, it can shatter your composure as you try to come up with an answer on the spot, and your sudden increase in anxiety can turn your prospect off and cost you the sale. In contrast, if you've anticipated their objection, scripted an answer, and rehearsed your script, you can come back with a smooth, confident response that will impress your prospect and increase their confidence in buying from you.

Build Your Confidence with Scripting Affirmations

In order to internalize the new ideas about scripting I've taught in this chapter and make these beliefs about scripting part of your habitual mindset, I recommend you practice repeating the key points in this chapter as affirmations. Here are some examples of affirmations you can repeat based on the material in this chapter:

> *A script is a series of words in sequence that has meaning.*
>
> *I'm already using scripts subconsciously.*
>
> *Conscious scripting makes my presentations more effective.*
>
> *Sales scripting is the most powerful way for me to improve my presentation results.*
>
> *Scripting is preparation.*
>
> *Scripting overcomes anxiety.*
>
> *Scripting builds confidence.*

Practice repeating each of these affirmations seven times, every day for a month, and notice how it changes your feelings about scripting.

Exercise

For the next month, practice repeating each of these scripting affirmations seven times, and notice how your feelings about scripting change as a result:

A script is a series of words in sequence that has meaning.

I'm already using scripts subconsciously.

Conscious scripting makes my presentations more effective.

Sales scripting is the most powerful way for me to improve my presentation results.

Scripting is preparation.

Scripting overcomes anxiety.

Scripting builds confidence.

Ideas Into Action

Arvee Robinson is one of my star students. I met Arvee at a seminar many years ago. At the time she was struggling in her business. She was uncomfortable selling and uncomfortable with sales scripting. She really connected with my message, however, of teaching people how to sell from honesty, integrity, and compassion. Arvee signed up for my program and I started to work with her. Arvee responded very well to my material and made a conscious decision to embrace sales, embrace sales scripting, and take massive action.

Arvee's income had gone from about $4,000 a month, to where she now regularly earns $15,000 to $20,000 a month. My vision for Arvee is that one day she'll earn over $100,000 in a single month. Arvee is a fantastic public speaking trainer and she has my full endorsement. If you are looking to grow your business giving speeches, go to www.instantprospeaker.com to see how Arvee Robinson can help you.

Key Points Review

■ Scripting works because human beings respond in predictable ways.

■ A script is a series of words in sequence that have meaning.

■ Whether you think you're using scripts or not, you are using scripts.

■ Sales scripting is the most powerful way for you to improve your presentation results.

■ Preparation is the best antidote for anxiety.

■ Use sales scripting affirmations to embrace scripting and build confidence.

Chapter 2

Breaking through Scriptwriter's Block

Can you remember a time back in school where you had to complete a long writing assignment? Maybe you had to turn in a 10-page essay at mid-term. Or maybe you had to write a five-paragraph essay for a test that was due at the end of class. Did you ever find yourself staring at the blank page wondering what you were going to write? Can you remember what it was like worrying about trying to finish in time before your writing assignment was due? Did you feel the anxiety mounting minute by minute as the deadline drew closer?

All of us have these kinds of memories buried in our subconscious, and I've found they can come back to haunt people when they start trying to write sales scripts. Just as writers can get writer's block, sales script writers can get "scriptwriter's block." I struggled with writer's block myself when I was writing my first full-length book, *The System*. Even though I'd had years of experience writing sales scripts, I found myself putting the book project off for nearly a decade until I finally made a commitment to complete it. When I finally made that commitment, the book got done and became an Amazon bestseller, which launched my company to new levels of success. I could've enjoyed that success years earlier if I hadn't let writer's block slow me down.

Scriptwriter's block might be holding back your success, too. For many people, the anxiety associated with scriptwriter's block can be a barrier to embracing scriptwriting. To help you get past this problem, I've borrowed some techniques that professional writers use to defeat writer's block in order to meet their deadlines, and I've adapted them to beating scriptwriter's block. In this chapter I'm going to share four simple but powerful techniques you can use to break through scriptwriter's block.

Schedule Time to Write

One of the time management distinctions I teach is that what doesn't get scheduled doesn't get done. When I talk about this I'm usually applying it to sales activity such as scheduling time to generate leads, but the same principle also applies to scheduling time to work on your sales scripts. The first step to breaking through scriptwriter's block is setting an intent to write, which means committing a definite block of your time to writing.

Part of the secret to persuading yourself to make this kind of commitment is to limit the amount of writing time you schedule to something you find manageable. If you visualize writing for hours on end, you're going to dread the idea of sitting down to write, and you're going to procrastinate. Instead, schedule small, bite-sized chunks of time where you can work in brief but intense bursts of activity.

One method some professional writers use is setting a timer to limit their writing time. You can set the time for ten, fifteen, twenty, or thirty minutes. When the timer goes off, stop working and take a break. This will give you a chance to renew your energy. Avoid the temptation to skip your break, because this will wear you out, and you'll start to associate writing with feeling worn out, which will make you want to procrastinate.

When you use this method, be sure to set up a comfortable work environment to make your writing experience positive and productive. Choose a location where you can get away from distractions. Don't get sidetracked by phones, texting, or email. Use a comfortable chair, a notebook or computer screen that's easy to see and read, and an input device you find comfortable. If you don't like to type, you might consider recording your voice using speech-to-text software to create the first draft of your script, or you can hire a transcriber.

One way I help my students put this technique into practice is by offering virtual scriptwriting classes and workshops with time blocked out for working on scripts. I share scriptwriting techniques, then give my students some time to apply the information to their own scripts, and follow up by providing some review time where participants' scripts can receive feedback from me, my coaching team, and fellow students. To learn more about the scriptwriting opportunities I offer, visit the page for my Gold Protege Program:

http://goldprotege.com/

Start Easy with a Simple Script

When you're learning a language, you learn how to pronounce and write the letters of the alphabet before you start trying to write words and sentences. When you're learning math, you learn to count to ten before tackling negative numbers or fractions. When you're learning piano, you start by learning notes and scales before trying to play songs. In any field, you learn by starting with the basics and gradually working up to more advanced material. It's the same way with learning sales scripts. The easiest way to learn is by starting with a simple script.

In Chapter 4 I'm going to talk about how to pick which script to work on first, and one of the options I suggest is picking the script that you'll find easiest to finish. If you're struggling with scriptwriter's block, this is the best option to help you to get started. You can pick an easy script for practice to build your skills and confidence. This will give you a foundation for writing more challenging scripts.

You can choose a script that you already need to write, or if none of your scripts seem easy enough to practice on, you can select a short, simple script format for practice. Examples of short scripts are social media private messages, posts, and comments; emails; phone calls to make introductions or schedule appointments; and elevator pitches. Later in this book I'll give you tips for how to write each of these formats and others, but right now the important thing is not to write a perfect script, but to pick something simple enough to motivate yourself to get started. We'll worry about polishing up your script later, but right now we're just trying to get you to start practicing.

Use Starter Templates

If I asked you to draw a picture of the Mona Lisa, unless you've had some artistic training, you might not feel confident about how your drawing would turn out. But if I gave you a children's connect-the-dots drawing or coloring book and asked you to complete a drawing, you would find that easy to do. Having a template to work from makes it easy to get started.

In a similar way, you can use sales script templates to get started on scripts. In the following chapters of this book I'm going to give you a universal template you can apply to any sales script, based on the universal steps in the sales process. I call these steps "Sales Mountain," as covered in my book *The System* and in my Silver Protege Program. In my Gold Protege program I teach my students how to write scripts that correspond to each of the steps in the sales process. These steps serve as a template you can use to outline the sequence of any sales script. I'll teach you these steps in the following chapters so you can use them as a template to help you write your scripts.

In addition to this universal template, which applies to all sales scripts in general, you can also find templates for specific types of sales scripts and parts of sales scripts. For example, the classic copywriting formula for writing ads follows a four-part script known as "AIDA," which stands for "Attention, Interest, Desire, Action." The AIDA formula provides copywriters with a template for outlining ads. If you start studying the wording of ads and how their structure is sequenced, you'll start to see the same patterns used over and over in ads on the Internet, TV, radio, newspapers, magazines, and other media. These will give you many examples of how to use templates to write scripts. Later in this book I'll share some templates you can use for writing different types of scripts.

Fill in the Blanks

Once you have a template, finishing your script becomes a matter of filling in the blanks. Think of a crossword puzzle or the TV show Wheel of Fortune, which is based on the paper-and-pencil game Hangman. In Hangman you start with a template consisting of dashes, representing how many letters you need to fill in. Each time you guess a letter correctly, your opponent fills in all the dashes where that letter occurs. The more letters you fill in, the easier it becomes to guess the word. If you're strategic about picking letters that occur most frequently in English, such as the letters "E," "T," and "A," your odds of guessing the word go up higher than if you were guessing randomly.

You can use a "fill-in-the-blanks" strategy to help you complete your sales scripts as well. Modern advertising has been around for over a century, and no matter what your product or service is, the odds are very high that either someone has already written a script very similar to what you need, or someone has written a script close enough to what you need that you can borrow a piece of it for your purposes and combine it with pieces of other scripts. Professional copywriters apply this strategy by collecting a "swipe file" of other writers' successful ads they can adapt when writing new ads. I learned some of the successful scripts used by public speakers when I was working for Dante Perano and Tony Robbins. You can borrow the scripts I use in my presentations and on my websites, and you can add other scripts to your personal swipe file by studying other successful sales script. I'll include some sample scripts in Chapter 13.

Exercise

Pick a short, simple script you can work on for practice. Schedule ten to thirty minutes of time you can work on it. Find an example of a similar script you can use for a swipe file to help you get started.

What script will I work on? _____

When will I work on it? _____

Where can I find an example of a similar script for a swipe file? _____

_____

Ideas Into Action

Mark Tosoni (**www.marktosoni.com**) has been teaching how to sell alarms for over two decades. During that period he has made extensive use of sales scripting. Mark writes, "I've been using sales scripting for over two decades in the alarm systems business and can say with absolute certainty it has not only lead me to alarm sales mastery but has done the same for anyone who dares to engage in this sales discipline. I can directly attribute sales scripting to the sales of tens of thousands of alarm accounts, to the tune of multi-million-dollar sales figures every year without fail. We are creatures of habit, and having a strategic presentation laid out from start to finish is the most intelligent thing any sales pro can do. Eric Lofholm is the absolute authority on this subject, and anyone who is serious about results should say yes to anything Eric is offering as that will equal automatic sales increase. I'm glad I did!"

Key Points Review

- Schedule short blocks of writing time to overcome the tendency to procrastinate on scriptwriting.

- Start with simple scripts for practice to overcome the intimidation factor.

- Use starter templates to help you get your scripts started.

- Use swipe files to help you complete your templates by filling in the blanks.

PART II

The Outer Game
of Sales Scripting

In Part Two, I'm going to share with you my formula for writing a successful sales script. Scripting has a step-by-step process, very similar to baking a recipe. My recipe for sales scripting has five key ingredients processed through a seven-step sequence:

1. Pick a script to write

2. Collect your five laundry lists

3. Identify your sales model

4. Outline your script

5. Write your script section by section

6. Persuasion engineer your script

7. Revise, improve, and update your script

The chapters in this section will cover each of these steps. They will also provide guidance on how to apply these steps to different types of scripts for specific formats such as face-to-face presentations, front-of-the-room talks, virtual talks, phone calls, email, social media, and multimedia formats. I'll show you how to find scripts you can borrow from, and I'll provide some sample scripts you can customize to create your own. Finally I'll give you a practical program for putting these steps into action to get your scripts written.

Chapter 3

The Scripting Process

To illustrate the process of scripting, imagine you were going to bake a cake. If you were going to bake a cake, you would start with a list of ingredients such as flour, sugar, and eggs. You would then prepare the ingredients by following a series of steps, starting by sifting the dry ingredients together, adding liquids, pouring the mixture in a pan, baking it, letting it cool, and adding frosting. If you follow these steps using the right ingredients in the right sequence, even someone with little cooking skill can bake a cake and have it turn out tasting pretty good. But if you substituted ketchup for eggs, your cake would have problems. And you wouldn't try putting the frosting on before mixing your ingredients together. Changing the ingredients or the steps turns an easy cake recipe into a big mess.

The sales scripting process can be as easy as baking a cake if you follow the recipe. You don't have to be a professional copywriter to write an effective sales script. You just need a desire to create an effective script and follow the system. What you do need are the right ingredients and the right steps so your scripting recipe can follow the right process. In this chapter I'm going to introduce you to the key ingredients and steps that make up my scripting process.

The Five Key Ingredients to Any Sales Script

The five ingredients for a sales script are based on the steps in a sales presentation. I discussed these steps in detail in my book *The System*, and I teach them in depth in my Silver Protege course. Many of you are already familiar with that material, but for those of you who are not, I describe the steps in the sales process as a "Sales Mountain," as illustrated in this diagram:

The Sales Mountain

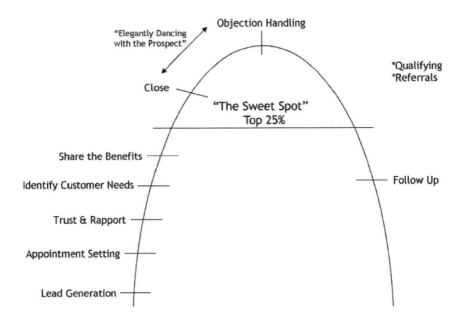

In the Sales Mountain sequence, lead generation and appointment setting precede the actual sales presentation. The presentation itself has these main steps:

1. Building trust and rapport
2. Identifying customer needs
3. Sharing benefits
4. Closing
5. Objection handling

There is then the additional step of following up, which comes after the actual presentation. I also include two "wild card" steps which can vary as to whether and where they appear in the sequence, qualifying and referrals.

From the five steps in the sales presentation sequence, we get five types of scripts for:

1. Stories

2. Probing questions

3. Benefits

4. Offer

5. Objections

These five types of scripts form the key ingredients to any sales presentation.

(Now some of you might be thinking, "But Eric, can't I write scripts for lead generation or appointment booking, too? What about follow-up? What about scripts for qualifying or referrals? And can't I use stories for any part of a sales presentation?" The answer is yes, and yes, and I'm oversimplifying for now to get the basic logic behind the five types of scripts across. But for those of you who are wondering, yes, you can write scripts for lead generation and appointment booking, but when you do, what you'll find is that they replicate the steps in a sales presentation, just in modified and often condensed form. For instance, if you're giving a lead generation talk, even if you're not trying to sell anything, you still want to open up by building trust and rapport, which is often done by using a story. And yes, you can use stories for other parts of the sales process besides building trust and rapport. For instance, you might tell a story to illustrate a benefit or handle an objection. But even though stories can be used for other purposes, stories are especially effective for building trust and rapport, and even when you use them for other purposes, they help you maintain trust and rapport. Because of this, to help you memorize the five types of scripts, it can help jog your memory to keep things simple for now and think of stories as associated with building trust and rapport, as long as you understand that's not their only potential use. The bottom line is that if you master the five key script ingredients, you can write scripts for any phase of the sales process.)

The Seven Key Steps to Writing any Sales Script

The number of ingredients in a recipe is often different than the number of steps it takes to prepare those ingredients. For instance, a peanut butter sandwich only has two ingredients, bread and peanut butter, but it takes three steps to lay the two slices of bread down, spread the peanut butter, and place one piece of bread on top of the other. In sales scripting, there are five key ingredients, but it takes seven steps to assemble those ingredients together. The seven steps are:

1. Pick a script to write
2. Collect your five laundry lists
3. Identify your sales model
4. Outline your script
5. Write your script section by section
6. Persuasion engineer your script
7. Revise, improve, and update your script

Picking a script involves prioritizing which of your sales scripts you should work on first. In the chapter on this I'll give you some strategies for deciding which scripts to prioritize.

Collecting your five laundry lists refers to assembling the five key ingredients that go into any sales script.

Identifying your sales model connects your script to the steps in your customized sales process so that you can design your script to support your sales process.

Outlining your script is mapping out the sequence of your script.

Writing your script section by section expands on your outline by filling in one piece of your script at a time to create a rough draft.

Persuasion engineering your script is editing your rough draft to make the language of your stories, questions, benefits, offers, and objection responses more persuasive.

Revising, improving, and updating your script involves tracking the results of your script deployment and making adjustments based on the feedback you get.

These are the steps involved in writing any sales script. All you have to do is follow this recipe and you can write sales scripts as easy as baking a cake.

Ideas into Action

Jeffrey Howard learned my sales script writing system in 2005. He sells by giving speeches, phone sales, and automated presentations like prerecorded messages and webinars. Jeffrey scripts out all of these presentations. As a result of implementing my sales script writing system, he has generated well over $100,000 in additional income. In addition, he has taught many of my ideas to his sales team. He has earned a lot of additional income in overrides from his team.

To put the ideas in this chapter into action, I'd like to suggest you take three main actions:

- First, commit to memorizing the five key ingredients and seven steps in the scripting process.

- Second, commit to studying the following chapters in this section to learn the seven scripting steps in more depth.

- Third, to help you get the most out of this book, check out my Gold Protege scripting program where you can get ongoing support putting the steps in my scripting program into practice:

http://goldprotege.com/

Key Points Review

- Sales scripting is like following a recipe.
- Sales scripts have five key ingredients.
- The sale scripting process has seven key steps.
- For additional sales scripting support, visit:

    http://goldprotege.com/

Chapter 4

Pick a Script to Write

Imagine you're a student back in high school and you're taking six classes, and you've got a homework assignment in each one. Which one do you do first? Six homework assignments at once could feel a bit overwhelming and your first reaction might be to feign illness and play hooky the next day. But of course if you did that, you'd just have twice as much homework to make up when you went back to school. So instead of letting your homework keep piling up, you'd eventually decide to tackle the problem, and you'd do this by asking yourself some practical questions. Which assignment can have the biggest impact on my grade? Which one is due first? Which one can I finish most easily? Answering these questions will help you decide which assignment to tackle first.

Picking a sales script to write involves a similar process. If you're lucky you've only got one script to worry about, but chances are you've got several, putting you in a situation similar to our hypothetical high school student. Fortunately, you can use a strategy similar to the one our student used in our example to help you decide which script to write first.

List Which Scripts You Need

The first step is to make a list of all the scripts you need. There are a few principles you can use to help you compile your list.

Which Products and Services Need Scripts?

One way to list your scripts is to list all the products and services you offer and identify which ones need scripts. If you sell multiple products or services, you may need several or even many scripts. In this case you might need to pick a few top-selling items to focus on. But you can narrow down which items to focus on later in the process. For now just get all your products and services listed.

Which Steps in Your Sales Process Need Scripts?

When selling any product or service, the steps in the Sales Mountain sales process apply, which provides another principle for assembling your script list. For each product or service, identify what steps in the sales process need scripting. Do you need lead generation scripts? Appointment setting scripts? Scripts for trust and rapport, probing questions, benefits, closing, or objection handling? Follow-up sales scripts? Qualifying scripts? Referral scripts?

Which Formats Need Scripts?

For any product or service or any step in the sales process, you can also craft scripts in multiple formats for different media. Examples of common formats include:

- Main sales presentations
- Networking elevator pitches
- Front-of-the-room presentations
- Webinars
- Teleconferences
- Phone calls and messages
- Texting
- Social media

- Website opt-in forms
- Email
- Direct mail
- Print ads
- Radio ads
- TV ads
- Video ads

Consider your most important promotional and sales strategies and use these to help you identify which media formats you need scripts for.

Prioritize Your List

After listing which scripts you need, you can rank your list in order of priority. Here are a few different ways you can rank your list.

By Value

All items on your list will not have equal revenue potential. For instance, if you have a high-priced product or service, that represents more revenue potential per sale than a lower-ticket item. A closing script is generally more essential to revenue generation than an objection-handling script, even though both are important. A script that enables you to generate hundreds or thousands of sales through social media represents more value than a script that only lets you make one face-to-face sale at the same price point.

By Deadline Urgency

Another way to prioritize your scripts is by urgency. For instance, if you've got a major sales opportunity coming up next week, getting the script for that presentation done in time may trump your other scripts in urgency.

By Ease of Completion

A third way to prioritize your scripts is by identifying which ones are easiest to complete. If you're struggling with scriptwriter's block, if you just feel overwhelmed by a big pile of scripts, or if you have some spare time, working on an easy script can be a way to clear some items off your plate.

Pick Which Script to Write

Based on how you've prioritized your scripts, you should pick one script to start writing. This is the key to getting started and moving from thinking about scripting to actually doing it.

If you get excited and you're feeling ambitious, you may feel tempted to pick several scripts. Nine times out of ten, this will result in you dividing your attention and getting less done than if you had committed to one script. Make a decision to finish a single script and then stick with it until it's complete. Your other scripts will still be waiting for you when you're done and you can pick another one to work on then.

Exercise

1. List all the scripts you need written, considering different products and services, sales steps, and media formats.
2. Prioritize your list according to which scripts are most valuable, most urgent, or easiest to complete.
3. Based on your priorities, pick one script to work on first.

Ideas Into Action

Rosie Bank is in health coaching, executive wellness, and direct marketing. Before training with me, she had never received professional sales training. Rosie began training with me in 2010. She says that in addition to increasing her close ratio, training with me has also given her a huge boost in confidence stemming from the knowledge that people will buy her products and services. Rosie writes, "I think of what I learned from Eric practically every day. Some of his strategies (sales funnel, Sales Mountain) are timeless. The more I use them, the more I appreciate them."

Key Points Review

- Start by listing which scripts you need.
- Prioritize your scripts by which scripts are most valuable, most urgent, or easiest to complete.
- Pick a script to start writing.

Chapter 5

Collect Your Five Laundry Lists

In the days before most homes had electricity and washing machines, many people sent their wash to commercial laundry services. Workers at these services marked the clothes for identification, then sorted the loads of clothing by material and color. As the workers marked and sorted the clothes, they recorded the marks and quantities on a list of categories of clothing for reference. This list enabled them to make sure everything got washed, identify any missing items, and return clean clothes back to their owners. This is where we got the term "laundry list." Today the term has become a metaphor referring to any long list of items that need to be done.

When I teach sales scripting, I use a laundry list that sorts scripts into five categories, based on the steps in a sales presentation. After you've picked a script to write, the next step is to start collecting the laundry list of items that go with that script. Each of these items constitutes a smaller script or "subscript" that forms part of your full sales presentation script. You can then assemble the pieces together when delivering your actual presentation. Extending the laundry analogy, you can think of the items on your list as parts of your wardrobe you can mix and match. Just as you can wear the same pair of socks with different pants and shirts, you can combine the same story with different probing questions or benefits when addressing different audiences, for example.

Sorting your script components this way lets you work on one piece of your script at a time, making them easier to write and memorize. It also lets you combine your script components in customized ways during live presentations, which is why you can still be spontaneous even though you've rehearsed.

Let's take a closer look at the five laundry lists.

Stories

The first step in a sales presentation is building trust and rapport, and one of the best ways to do this is by telling stories. As I mentioned earlier, stories can also be used for other purposes, but they are especially effective for building trust and rapport, and they are one of my favorite sales techniques.

Why are stories so effective at building trust and rapport? Here are a few reasons.

1. Stories Move People Emotionally

Imagine the emotions associated with watching a movie. An action or thriller film can bring you to the edge of your seat. A comedy can make you laugh. A romantic movie can tug at your heart. A tragedy can make you cry. Movies elicit strong emotions because they bring stories to life. Stories can also arouse intense feelings during a sales presentation, which can help you motivate someone to take action.

2. Stories Act as Invisible Selling

Stories can deliver a message without being obvious about it by cloaking the point in metaphors. The parables of Jesus are a famous example. In the Parable of the Sower, Jesus used farming as a metaphor to describe how different types of people would respond to his message. In response to the question, "Who is my neighbor?", Jesus answered with the story of the Good Samaritan. He used the Parable of the Prodigal Son to teach how God welcomes sinners home. Aesop's Fables are another famous example. I use Aesop's story of "The

Tortoise and the Hare" to illustrate how persistence in consistency triumphs over the long run. In modern times, sales masters such as Earl Nightingale, Glenn Turner, and Jim Rohn have used parables and fables effectively. Stories let you sell without looking like you're selling.

3. Stories Suspend Time

Did you ever have a dream that seemed to go on for hours or days, and then you woke up to find it was still the middle of the night? Or did you ever get so absorbed in a movie or a book that by the time you finished, you were surprised how much time had passed? A good story pulls the audience out of real time into a different time zone defined by the imagination. This is useful for a sales presentation when you're trying to get someone to forget about other things they have on their busy schedule and get them to stop watching the clock and focus on your presentation.

4. Stories Can Increase Rapport

Rapport is created when one person starts experiencing feelings and thoughts similar to those of another person. Stories promote rapport in several ways. When you start listening to a story, it tunes your auditory awareness into the pace of their voice. As you hear their words echo in your mind, you start to visualize the images painted by their words. You may start to visualize one of the characters in their story, and you may even start to imagine things from the perspective of that character and feel what that character feels. All of these factors combine to build rapport between you and the storytellers.

5. Stories Can be Humorous

"I have a switch in my apartment," deadpan comedian Steven Wright recounted. "It doesn't do anything. Every once in a while, I turn it on and off. One day I got a call. It was from a woman in France. She said, 'Cut it out.'"

Humorous stories can draw your audience in. You use funny stories from your own experience, jokes, puns, irony, and other humorous elements to amuse your audience and make them smile and laugh. Humor relaxes your audience, which can help take the tension out of your sales presentation.

Probing Questions

The next item on the laundry list is probing questions. Probing questions are questions you use to identify the needs of your prospect. They set the stage for the rest of your presentation by tapping into what your prospect really wants. Because of this, improving your probing questions, is the fastest way for you to increase the persuasiveness of your presentation.

A good probing question digs below the surface to uncover the prospect's hidden needs.

Here are some examples of probing questions:

> *What type of budget do you have to work with?*
> *How soon would you like to get started?*
> *Have you ever worked with a realtor before?*
> *Where do you currently buy your office supplies?*

By rewording questions as statements in command form, you can also create probing statements, such as these:

> *Tell me about your situation.*
> *Describe to me your dream job.*

I teach my sales students to prepare for a presentation by thinking of the most powerful questions they could ask the prospect. One exercise to help you do this is making a list of five questions and statements you can potentially use during your presentation.

Benefits

The next laundry list item is benefits. Benefits are the value your prospect gets from buying what you sell. For instance, someone who buys fast food might be anticipating the taste when they get it in their mouth, or the feeling when they get it in their stomach. When someone is considering buying something, they weigh the benefit against the price and other risks. For instance, in the fast food example, they might wonder if the taste satisfaction they're going to receive is worth the financial price or the cost to their health and self-esteem from gaining weight. Weighing benefits against risks is kind of like a mental teeter-totter in your prospect's mind. On one side of the teeter-totter is price, on the other is value. Benefits help you stack more weight on the value side of the teeter-totter.

I teach that there are five different types of benefits:

- Tangible benefits
- Intangible benefits
- The benefit of taking action
- The consequences of not taking action
- Benefit of the benefit

Tangible benefits are physical or measurable things like saving you money, making you money, decreasing employee turnover, and so on.

Intangible benefits are difficult to touch or measure, yet are still appealing. Intangible benefits include things like greater peace of mind, increased confidence, and so on. You can't always quite put your finger on intangible benefits, but they're very real benefits that people want.

The benefit of taking action is closely linked with the benefit of *the consequences of not taking action.* When I encourage people to create sales scripts, I let them know that the benefit of taking action by creating sales scripts is that they will close at a higher ratio, and thus make more money. The consequence of not taking action is that, for every presentation you deliver without having an effective sales script, you leave money on the table.

The benefit of the benefit is often the real reason why people buy. It is associated with the more obvious benefits of purchasing, but the association may be indirect, unstated, or even unconscious. For instance, when I'm selling sales training, I may say to a prospect, "Imagine you are now a sales champion. How will your life be different? What kind of car will you be driving?" They will usually say something like, "Oh, when I am a sales champion, I'll be driving this kind of car." In this example, one of the benefits of being a sales champion is that you make more sales. And then the benefit of the benefit of making more sales is you make more money. And the benefit of the benefit of the benefit is that you could drive the car that you want. So there is a chain of association between the overt benefit and the underlying benefit of the benefit.

Offer

The next piece of your script is your offer, which is the part of your script that goes with your close. The close is the section of the presentation where you ask for commitment. The close is the natural conclusion to a well delivered presentation. The heavy lifting is actually done in the body of the presentation. At the end of the presentation where you are closing, you are simply leading and guiding the prospect to the next step.

I teach my students to break the sequence of their close down into three sections:

1. The transition into the close
2. The body of the close
3. The final, final close

The transition into the close bridges between the previous part of your sales presentation and the offer you're about to extend. You can achieve this shift by using a transitional phrase such as, "What I'd like to do now is extend you an opportunity to work with me one-on-one as one of my coaching clients."

The body of the close conveys the details of your offer, such as:

- Name of the product or service
- Price
- What's included
- Length of contract
- Incentive for buying today
- Method of payment
- Terms of payment
- Bonuses
- Guarantees
- Warrantees

The body of your close can include as many of these elements as apply to your offer. Together these elements form a mini laundry list.

The final, final close is the part of your close where you conclude with a call to action. "Would you like to buy some Girl Scout Cookies?"

I teach my students a full arsenal of closing techniques. For instance, in the "Ask and Be Silent Close," you ask for a commitment and then remain silent as you await a response. In the "Assumption Close," you ask a question or make a statement assuming the sale has been made, using a phrase such as, "Which credit card would you like to use today?" In the "Alternate of Choice Close," you offer a pair of options which both assume a sale, using a phrase such as, "We accept Visa, American Express, Discover, or MasterCard. Which card would you like to use?" The "Scarcity Close" emphasizes the consequences of not taking action by using a phrase such as, "We only have one left. Would you like to get it?" I cover many other closing techniques in my book *The System* and in my sales training courses.

I teach a simple three-step formula for writing closing scripts:

1. Make a laundry list of the components of your close (transition into close, name of product or service, price, what's included, final final close, etc.)

2. Put the components in order to create a closing outline

3. Write a mini-script for each section of the outline

Following this formula creates the script for your offer.

Objections

The final scripting category is scripts for objection handling. Objection handling is sort of like mental chess. Part of chess is anticipating your opponent's move. I do not view sales as a competition against the prospect but the concept is a useful way to understand the importance of preparing for objections your prospect might voice.

Objection handling is a form of negotiation. An example is when you go to buy a used car. The dealer might open with a $25,000 offer, and you might come back with an $18,000 offer. You then negotiate until you reach a mutually-agreeable price point.

There are typically seven to twelve common objections in any industry. This is great news because it means you have a limited number of common objections to prepare for. By rehearsing how you might respond to these objections, you can improve your objection-handling ability.

Here are some examples of common objections that arise in most industries in one form or another:

1. I need to think about it.
2. I don't have any money.
3. I need to talk it over with someone.
4. Can you send me some information?
5. I don't have the time.
6. Your price is too high.
7. I am already working with someone.
8. We already tried it and it didn't work.
9. I am not interested.

Often these objections reflect a deeper, non-stated objection which is the true objection. For instance, someone might not have been convinced of the value of your product when you were conveying its benefits, and this might lead them to see your offer as a waste of time, prompting them to say, "I don't have the time," when the real, underlying problem is that they don't see the value. These types of invisible objections are often the ones that cost you the most sales.

I teach my sales students over a dozen techniques for handling objections. One way is to tell a story about a prospect who had a similar objection and became a buyer anyway. Another way is to ask questions to bring out the unstated objection. A third way is to solve the problem that creates the objection, for instance by offering a low monthly payment plan to solve the problem of a high price objection. A fourth way is to address the objection earlier in your presentation before it ever surfaces. I cover many more techniques in my book *The System* and in my Silver Protege training program.

Exercise

Using a computer or paper, create a folder for the script you've picked to write. Inside that folder, create documents for each of the five script categories that make up your laundry lists. If you have any pre-existing sales scripts or materials, you can copy them into the folder or copy their contents into your documents.

Ideas Into Action

Lauren Supraner works for a company that provides intercultural and language training to multicultural organizations, targeting professionals in large international corporations in the STEM fields (science, technology, engineering, mathematics). Before studying my system, she had never received professional sales training, and had spent 10 years doing speeches about accent reduction for foreign-born professionals without gaining a single client as a result. She recently began using my scripting method to create scripts for her accent reduction product and for cultural competency training for healthcare providers. She describes the results she got as "striking." She recently spoke to the Sino-American Pharmaceutical Association, for the first time viewing her speech as an opportunity to sell to everyone in the room of 200 instead of just giving a talk for exposure. Her presentation generated $10,000 in sales, along with 15 leads, several contacts with persons of influence, two onsite classes at a large pharmaceutical company, and invitations to speak at an SAPA conference at MIT and a Chinese-American Chemistry Society at Rutgers. The ripple effect of the conference also attracted a new private student, a renewal of a corporate training commitment, and additional speaking opportunities, including overseas speaking engagements. Lauren writes, "This small (yet huge) change in my delivery has opened doors and had a ripple effect beyond the one-time presentation. I now have a strategy to continue growing in this way. Because I changed the presentation towards sales, I have also made great inroads into the pharmaceutical industry (big target market) rather than just a one-time speaking engagement."

Key Points Review

- Sales scripts are made up of five categories of scripts that form "five laundry lists."

- The five laundry lists are: stories, probing questions, benefits, offers, objections.

- Story scripts help build trust and rapport with your prospects, and can also serve other functions.

- Probing question scripts help you identify prospect needs.

- Benefit scripts make your prospects want to buy from you.

- Offer scripts close your sale.

- Objection scripts prepare you to address prospect concerns.

- For each script you pick to write, assemble your five laundry lists.

Chapter 6

Identify
Your Sales Model

The success of the Gillette razor company is a great case study in the importance of sales models. Company founder King Gillette became famous for popularizing one of the most successful sales models of all time: the free giveaway or "freebie" marketing, also known as the "razors and blades" sales model. As he was developing the disposable razor, Gillette realized that the real profit potential in his idea was not the razors themselves, which the consumer only had to buy once, but the disposable blades, which consumers had to buy again and again. Leveraging this fact, Gillette offered his razors at a cheap price in order to make money from the blades, adopting the motto, "Give 'em the razor; sell 'em the blades." Within a few years Gillette became a millionaire, and today, over a century later, the company he left behind is worth an estimated $16 billion. His freebie marketing sales model proved so successful that almost every industry employs it in some form or another today.

When you combine a good sales model with a good sales script, you get great results. A good sales script is designed to walk your prospect step-by-step through the steps in your sales model. But in order to design your script to achieve this, you first need to identify the steps in your sales model.

The Benefits of Identifying Your Sales Model

When I give a front-of-the-room speech or a webinar, I can predict with a high degree of confidence how many sales I'm going to generate. If I know how many people are in the room, I know from the experience of giving the same presentation many times what percentage of them are going to buy, and I know my price point, so all I have to do is crunch the numbers to predict the results. This gives me revenue consistency from one month to the next.

Contrast this with what would happen if I used a different sales model every time I gave a talk. Let's say that one time I gave my talk I told potential buyers to come up to the front of the room after my talk if they wanted to register for my program, but the next time I told them to call me, and the next time I told them to email me, and the next time I told them to visit my website. Could I consistently predict my results? Of course not. I'd be guessing about my results each and every time, and I'd have no confidence in how my business was going to perform from month to month.

The most effective way to create revenue consistency is to establish a sales model or process. Establishing a sales model lets you predict your revenue results with confidence. It also gives you the ability to test different parts of your sales process and make adjustments to improve its efficiency. For instance, I can test whether I get more registrations from a presentation by putting registration forms at a table or handing them out to audience members in their seats.

Types of Sales Models

Your sales model is defined by what you do with a lead after it comes in. For example, when I was a sales trainer for Tony Robbins, I would receive a referral such as an agent at a real estate office, and my job was to call that referral to book an appointment to be a guest speaker at an upcoming sales meeting. After the speech was scheduled, the next step was having what we called a "boss talk" with the meeting's coordinator to confirm the upcoming speech and discuss details, such as whether it was okay for me to sell from the front of the room at the end of my speech. Then there was the speech itself. Finally when the speech resulted in a sale, there was a follow-up procedure to process the sale. Each step in this process had its own script.

Over the years, a number of sales models have proven successful enough to become popular:

- The *one-call close* is illustrated by the Girl Scout Cookie sales model, where the sales representative asks for the order at the end of the first appointment.

- The *set appointment/one-call close* model is illustrated by real estate agents seeking listings, who first set an appointment and then attend the appointment and ask for the close at the end of the appointment.

- The *set appointment/one-call/two-call close* model is illustrated by some financial advisors who first set an appointment, then attend the appointment, and finally follow up with a second appointment where they ask for the close.

Other sales models and variations of these sales models exist. For instance, direct mail marketers have long used a variation of the set appointment/one-call close where they place an ad offering a free giveaway to generate leads, then respond to the leads with a sales pitch included in the giveaway. This is often followed up by additional direct mail sales efforts, becoming a variation on the set appointment/one-call/two-call close model. Internet marketers have adapted these models to online sales by using opt-in offers to build mailing lists.

Mapping Your Sales Model

What is your sales model? For instance, do you follow up an initial lead with a live visit, a letter, a phone call, or an email? What is the intended outcome of that follow-up procedure, and what is the next step and intended outcome? Once you make a sale, how do you follow up to deliver the product? How do you follow up to generate repeat business? How do you follow up to generate referrals?

The best way to map out the steps in your sales model is to "reverse engineer" it. This means starting with the desired outcome and then working back step-by-step to the initial lead to identify the steps in the process.

Exercise

Map out the steps in your sales model by following these steps:

    1. Identify the ultimate outcome or outcomes of your sales process.

    2. Identify your initial lead generation systems.

    3. Fill in the steps between your initial leads and the result of your sales process.

Ideas Into Action

One of my star clients, Doak Belt, is in financial services, and I am a client of his. Doak, who has a very interesting referral system, called me one day and said, "Eric, I am growing my business right now with referrals, and it would really mean a lot to me if you'd help me with some referrals. What I'd like to do is schedule a time where we can spend ten or fifteen minutes on the phone when you are in front of your database on your computer. Would you be willing to help me out?" He then set a referral appointment with me.

When Doak called for our phone meeting, he began by educating me on what a good referral was for him. "Eric," he said, "I am looking for small business owners that are homeowners and who are married with children. I also want to work with people who you think would be fun for me to work with."

I gave Doak three names. After I gave him each name, he said, "Eric, do you have the mailing address of this referral?"

I was a little confused. "Doak, I've never had someone ask me for a mailing address when asking for a referral. Why do you want their mailing address?"

"Well, once I have their contact and their mailing address, I put them in my database," Doak replied. "Then I send the referral a letter prior to calling them, letting the referral know that, in your case, 'Eric referred you to me,' and to be expecting my phone call."

"Doak, that's great. Why do you do that?"

"Well, in half the cases, the person that was the referral will call you up and say, 'I got this letter from this guy Doak, is he the real deal?'"

I later learned that two of the three referrals I gave Doak that day became his clients. Since then, Doak has scheduled three other referral appointments with me.

The idea behind a system is that you do it over and over and over again. So when you are thinking about leads, think in terms of a Lead Generation System.

Key Points Review

- The most effective way to create revenue consistency is to establish a sales model or process.

- Your sales model is defined by what you do with a lead after it comes in.

- Popular sales models include the *one-call close, set appointment/one-call close*, and the *set appointment/one-call/two-call close*.

- The best way to identify your sales model is to start with the desired outcome and reverse engineer the previous steps that lead from your initial lead to the final sale.

Chapter 7

Outline Your Script

When a home building company is getting ready to build a home, they have an architect draw a blueprint with detailed plans before they order materials and begin construction. This lets the building designers test ideas before building, saving the time and expense that it would cost to build something first, make a mistake, and then have to rebuild it. Artists often use a similar approach, starting with a rough sketch of stick figures to arrange the basic layout of a picture before adding details, inks, and colors. Writers also often start with a rough draft, typically in the form of an outline.

Applying the same principle, I teach outlining for sales script writing. Outlining lets you plan the sequence of your script so that it follows the optimal order of a persuasive sales presentation. You can adjust the main flow of your script before working on the details of each section. You can then write and edit each section individually. This approach makes the sequence of your script more persuasive, and it also makes it easier to write and edit each section as its own unit without having to revise your whole script. Outlining is the easiest way to get an effective script started.

Customizing Sales Mountain

The sequence of your outline is based on the steps in the sales process, which I sum up by using the image of Sales Mountain. I cover the steps in Sales Mountain extensively in my book *The System* and in my Silver Protege course, and I touched on it in Chapter 3 on the scripting process, but in case this material is still new to you, I'll give you a brief overview here.

In any industry, there are three keys to growing any business:

1. Lead generation
2. Appointment setting
3. Lead conversion

These three systems follow a logical sequence:

- Lead generation is making contact with people who want to buy from you
- Appointment setting is creating opportunities to deliver sales presentations to people who want to buy from you
- Lead conversion is delivering sales presentations

If we break down the process of lead conversion and include lead generation and appointment setting, we can divide the process of making a sale into eight steps. To help my students visualize and memorize these eight steps, I call them "climbing Sales Mountain."

The Sales Mountain

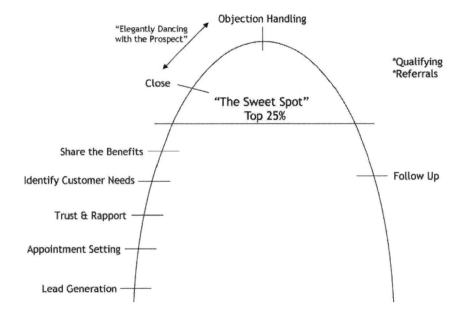

Here are the eight steps in Sales Mountain:

1. Lead generation
2. Appointment setting
3. Building trust and rapport
4. Identifying customer needs
5. Sharing benefits
6. Closing
7. Objection handling
8. Following up

If you look at the Sales Mountain diagram, you will also notice there are two "extra" steps with asterisks next to them, bringing the total from eight to ten steps:

- Qualifying
- Referrals

These last two items have asterisks because they are "wild cards" with special properties that can affect their inclusion and order in the sequence. With respect to qualifying, not all products and services require qualifying. For instance, if I'm inviting people to a free seminar, everyone is welcome, there's no need to qualify. On the other hand, if I'm selling a $10,000 coaching program I need to qualify the person to avoid wasting both of our time.

With respect to referrals, referrals can be incorporated into any step in the sales process, making their place in the sequence flexible. This is why referrals are also a wild card.

I'll dig more into the details of Sales Mountain as we cover how to script each of these steps in the next chapter. For now this is a brief overview to help you connect the Sales Mountain process to the structure of your script outline.

Roughing out Your Outline

To connect Sales Mountain to your outline, the first step is to use the steps in the Sales Mountain sequence to number the top level of your outline. In traditional outlining, you use Roman numerals to represent the top levels of your outline, then capital letters to represent the next levels down, followed by regular numerals, and so on, like this:

I. Top level
    A. Second level
        1. Third level
        2. Third level
    B. Second level
        1. Third level
        2. Third level
II. Top level
    A. Second level
        1. Third level
        2. Third level
    B. Second level
        1. Third level
        2. Third level

Today's word processing programs allow you to use variations on this traditional system that don't necessarily use Roman numerals, but the basic concept is the same.

If you apply this method to Sales Mountain, you would get something like this for your top levels of scripts:

I. Lead generation
II. Appointment setting
III. Lead conversion
    A. Building trust and rapport = story scripts
    B. Identifying customer needs = probing question scripts
    C. Sharing benefits = benefit scripts
    D. Closing = offer scripts
    E. Objection handling = objection scripts
    F. Following up

You can now see more clearly how the five laundry lists we discussed earlier fit into the big picture. Inserting the five laundry lists into this outline structure is how you start to rough out your script outline.

When actually applying this, you will need to customize the basic template to fit your specific sales model. For instance, if you have a sales model that involves a second follow-up appointment, you will need to include both appointments in the appointment-setting section of the outline.

Filling in Your Outline

The next step is filling in your outline by expanding the lower levels of your laundry list scripts. For instance, if I'm giving a lead generation speech, it might contain these sublevels:

   I. Lead generation

     A. Intro

     B. Outcomes

     C. Chunk 1

     D. Chunk 2

     E. Chunk 3

     F. Call to action

After some further refinement, this might look like this:

   I. Lead generation

     A. Intro

     B. My story

     C. Outcomes

        1. First outcome: Add value

        2. Second outcome: Invite you to participate in my program

     D. Drop the pen exercise

     E. Three ways to elevate your sales results

   F. Chunk 1: Belief

      1. Definition of a belief

      2. Belief metaphor

      3. Roger Bannister story

      4. Joey Aszterbaum story

   G. Chunk 2: Goal setting

      1. John Goodard story

      2. Arvee Robinson story

      3. Ask for referrals

   H. Chunk 3: "What Level" exercise

    I. Call to action

      1. Describe the program

      2. What they will learn

      3. Price

      4. Bonuses

      5. Guarantee

      6. Drop sell

      7. Final call to action

To take another example, in the body of your presentation, the probing question section of your script might break down into several subsections, like this:

   B. Probing question script

      1. Asking permission to ask questions

      2. Question #1

      3. Question #2

      4. Question #3

      5. Review of answers

In a similar way, you can expand the other parts of your outline.

You can expand each level of your outline into as many sublevels as you want. In the next chapter we'll focus on what happens when you complete the lowest levels of the outline by filling the actual paragraphs and sentences of your scripts.

Exercise

Using this template, start creating an outline for one of your sales scripts, expanding on the lower levels as needed:

   I. Lead generation

  II. Appointment setting

 III. Lead conversion

     A. Building trust and rapport = story scripts

     B. Identifying customer needs = probing question scripts

     C. Sharing benefits = benefit scripts

     D. Closing = offer scripts

     E. Objection handling = objection scripts

     F. Following up

Ideas Into Action

Rick Silva teaches business networking and referral generation to business owners. He'd had some sales training before he began studying my system about ten years ago. Rick writes that since then, "I've set and had over 4,300 one-on-one coffee meetings with professionals in coffee shops. I have given hundreds of webinars and live talks and have used Eric's ideas in all of them. On the networking side of my business I have closed a few thousand sales in the last ten years generating over $1.5 million. I have used the same techniques in my wife's business the last four years. We help people invest in land. I have easily generated another $1.2 million in income from roughly 350 appointments and about 200 sales." Rick currently uses sales scripting for live presentations and webinars and for his home study course on business networking, which he offers at www.thescienceofbusinessnetworking.com.

Key Points Review

- Outlines let you plan your script to make the sequence more persuasive and make the pieces easier to write and edit.

- The sequence of your outline is based on the steps in Sales Mountain.

- Rough out your outline by using the steps in Sales Mountain to define the top two levels of your outline.

- Fill in your outline by expanding on the lower levels of your outline.

Chapter 8

Write Your Script Section by Section

"Rome wasn't built in a day," the saying goes. The Romans were great builders, and their great architectural achievements were built one section at a time. For instance, one of the first and most famous Roman roads was the Appian Way, which was crucial to the expansion of the Roman army because it connected the city of Rome to strategic military bases. The original section of the Appian Way was built in 312 BC and stretched about 132 miles through mosquito-infested marshland from Rome to the city of Capua, enabling the army to quickly deploy troops and supplies over terrain that would have been slow and treacherous to navigate without a road. The road was so well-constructed it was said you could not slide a knife between the cracks in the bricks. The original section of the Appian Way proved key to expanding the reach of the Roman military and securing crucial victories, so the Romans decided to continue adding sections as their power expanded. The Romans continued adding sections to the Appian Way until it reached 350 miles. The road was so well-engineered that in the 18th century Pope Pius VI was able to restore it for modern use. It was used in World War II, and to this day the Appian Way contains the longest section of straight road in Europe.

When you carefully build a sales script section by section, it can also serve you well for many years of enduring use. Focusing on one section at a time lets you write and edit in small, manageable chunks. One section at a time, brick by brick, you build your road to sales success.

Getting Started

For many people, the toughest part of scripting is getting started. Once you get started, you start to gain momentum, but first you have to make that initial move forward. Here are a few strategies I recommend to get yourself into action.

Motivate Yourself to Take Action

Think of the toughest script you have to write. Now think of the toughest section in that script. It might be the opening story, the close, the probing questions, or whatever part you find the most challenging.

Now imagine I said I was going to pay you $100 if you could complete a first draft of this section within seven days. It wouldn't have to be perfect, it would just need to be complete. Could you motivate yourself do it? I'm going to bet most of you would say, "Yes."

Now what if I said I was going to pay you $10,000 to complete it in seven days. Would that motivate you to do it? I'm pretty sure the answer is, "Yes."

Now imagine that it's twelve months from today and all your scripts are done. How much more money are you making? The answer is probably a lot more than $10,000, if improving your scripts gets you even a few more sales during that time period.

Now imagine it's ten years from now, and you've been earning the extra revenue from having your scripts done for ten years. How much more money would you have? How would your life be different? What kind of home would you have? What kind of car? What kind of lifestyle?

Use this mental exercise to help you motivate yourself to get your scripts started. Once your scripts are done, you can use them over and over to increase your income for the rest of your life. Plus you'll enjoy saving hundreds and thousands of hours and prep time and anxiety because you'll have your scripts done and you'll be ready to give your presentations.

Focus on Completion, Not Perfection

When you start writing your sales scripts, in order to get done and not fall into the trap of procrastination, I recommend focusing on completion instead of perfection. The first time you write a sales script, it's not going to be a literary masterpiece. The good news is, it doesn't need to be. It just needs to be complete in order for you to start using it to make more sales. You can always improve your script. But in order to improve it, you first need something to improve. So start by focusing on completing your script. Improving and perfecting it comes later in the process.

Start with Your Baseline Script

To get started, the easiest way is to start with what I call your "baseline script." In land surveying, a baseline is an east-west line drawn on a map as reference point to define all the other plots of land on the map. It's sort of like in algebra where you have the X axis that defines where 0 is. The location of the baseline determines where everything else is. In baseball, the term was adopted to define the shortest path between the bases and home plate. If a runner runs more than three feet outside the baseline to avoid being tagged, they get called out. Successful base runners must maintain awareness of where the baseline is.

In business, your baseline reference point represents everything that you are currently doing to generate the results you are producing. This includes your current sales scripts.

Start with getting the script you're already using documented on paper. The easiest way to do this is to record yourself and transcribe the recording. You can do this yourself or pay someone to transcribe it.

Borrow Someone Else's Script

If you're not already using a standard script, or if you find there are pieces missing from the one you're using, another way to get started is to borrow someone else's script. Find a successful script that includes the type of material you need in your script. Get it in written form by either finding it as a text document or recording and transcribing it. Use this to get your own script started. Make whatever adjustments you need to adapt the original script to your own purposes.

Label and File Your Scripts

In order to find your scripts again later, it's important to label and file them in a way that will be easy to organize. I recommend that for each of your scripts, you create a folder for each of your five laundry lists. Inside each folder, place the files for your scripts and mini-scripts. Give your files names that will make it easy to identify which script is in that file. With story scripts, I give each story a name that helps me identify that story. For client success stories, I name the story after the client. For example, my "Doak Belt story" file is named after my client Doak Belt, who went from earning $30,000 a year to $25,000 a month by applying the scripting techniques I'm teaching you in this book.

Writing Your Five Laundry Lists

As you start getting into action, one of the most profitable goals you can work towards is competing your five laundry lists. Completing your five laundry lists will give you the essential components for completing the main body of your presentation. They will also give you the building blocks for completing other parts of your sales scripts.

Writing Story Scripts

Learning to write story scripts is vital to your scripting success. In my main presentation, stories typically form 10 to 50 percent of the presentation. The reason I rely on stories so heavily is that stories add powerful benefits to your sales presentation. Stories move people emotionally. They act as invisible selling. They suspend time. They can increase rapport. They can be humorous.

You can use stories in just about any place in your sales sequence. Stories are great for building rapport, and when you're thinking about the Sales Mountain sequence, you should think of stories as one of the main techniques for building trust and rapport, which is the context I introduced stories in back in Chapter 3 when I introduced you to how the Sales Mountain sequence connects with scripting. But stories can also be used for any other part of the sales sequence. You can use stories in your sales presentation to dramatize probing questions, benefits, offers, and objections. For instance, to set the stage for your close, you can tell a story about someone who bought the product you're going to be selling during your close and the results they got. You can also use stories for lead generation or appointment booking or to follow up on a sales presentation. During my lead generation talks, I often use the story of how I went from being a cook at McDonald's to becoming one of the world's leading sales trainers.

You can create many different types of stories. Some stories you can add to your arsenal include:

- Rapport-building stories, such as short humorous stories
- Your own story
- Your company's story

- Stories of satisfied clients

- Stories of prospects who didn't buy from you and now regret it

- Pre-closing stories that "preframe" the sale by portraying people who bought the product or service you will be selling at the end of the presentation

- Pre-closing stories that move prospect a step closer to yes by painting a scene of what the benefits would be like if they bought your product

When you're creating a story, you can outline the structure of your story to help you plan the sequence. A basic story structure includes a beginning, a middle, and an end. The beginning normally sets the scene by introducing the setting and characters and the basic plot conflict, like with the classic fairy-tale opening "Once upon a time…" In a sales story the plot conflict usually resolves around the problem your prospect is trying to solve in order to achieve their goals. This challenge can be represented by a character in the story who your prospect can identify with or a situation they can relate to. The middle of the story can then introduce the solution that will help solve the problem. The end of the story shows the results after the problem has been solved.

Think of a classic weight loss ad "before and after" story for an example of a basic sales plot. At the beginning of the story the person is shown struggling with weight gain and the consequences of being overweight. Then the ad introduces the new diet pill or exercise program that is being portrayed as a solution to the person's problem. The end shows the results after they have used the product and lost weight.

After outlining the sequence of your stories, the next step is to write them down word for word. Writing them down word for word will help you improve the flow and language of your stories. It will also help you memorize your stories and practice your delivery.

Exercise

Make a list of stories you can tell.

Outline the sequence of one of your stories.

Write down the story word for word.

Writing Probing Question Scripts

The next item on your five laundry lists is your probing questions. What I teach my students to do here is to think of the most powerful questions you could ask your prospect prior to your appointment or presentation. Then when you meet the prospect, you've got your question prepared in advance. This preparation gives you a huge advantage over trying to make up your questions and answers on the spot.

For the sequence of your probing questions section, before asking any questions, it's a best practice to ask permission so that you don't come across as interrogating the prospect. Launching into your probing questions without asking permission can put the prospect on the defensive. Make a gentle transition into your probing questions by saying something such as, "For me to best help you, Mr. Prospect or Mrs. Prospect, I need to ask you a few questions. Would that be okay?" A variation on this might be, "Prior to meeting with you today, I wrote down a list of questions, and with your permission I would like to go over those questions with you and take notes. Would that be okay?" Based on my experience prospects will almost always say, "Yes," providing you have laid a foundation with trust and rapport.

After making the transition into your probing questions, the next part of your probing questions section is the questions themselves. Your questions are meant to be probing, or attempting to dig below the surface to discover their true needs. You can use both probing questions and probing statements, which are simply questions rephrased in statement or command form. An example of a probing question would be: "How much money do you have in your budget?" A probing statement uses a statement or command to elicit a more open-ended response: "Tell me about your current _____ situation."

Here are some examples of probing questions that you can ask:

> What type of budget do you have to work with?
> How soon would you like to get started?
> Have you ever worked with a realtor before?
> Where do you currently buy your office supplies?

Here are some examples of probing statements:

> Tell me about your situation.
> Describe to me your dream job.
> Describe your credit to me.

Your probing questions and statements should be customized to your business and situation. For instance, you obviously wouldn't ask a prospect about their credit history if you were selling paper clips. Similarly, when attempting to book an appointment over the phone, you might have probing questions designed to help you get past the secretary to the decision-maker, which can differ from the probing questions you would ask during your main sales presentation.

To start getting practice writing probing questions, a good exercise is to plan the questions you will use on your next sales presentation. After setting up your next sales appointment, identify the key questions you plan to ask them.

Researching your prospect's background prior to the presentation can help you develop some good questions. Do a search for their name, website, or LinkedIn profile, or for their company's page. Read about what they do and think about what their needs might be and how you might be able to help them.

Exercise

Think of a prospect you will make a presentation to shortly. Develop five probing questions you might ask them:

1. _____
2. _____
3. _____
4. _____
5. _____

For this same prospect, develop five probing statements:

1. _____
2. _____
3. _____
4. _____
5. _____

Writing Benefit Scripts

Your benefit scripts are crucial to making the transition between your probing questions and your close. Your probing questions identify what your prospect needs. Your benefits communicate that you have what they need. In your close you offer them what they need. Your benefit script lays a solid foundation for your close when it establishes that your product or service meets the needs identified in your probing question section.

There are five different types of benefits:

> *Tangible benefits*
>
> *Intangible benefits*
>
> *The benefit of taking action*
>
> *The consequences of not taking action*
>
> *Benefit of the benefit*

Tangible benefits are real, physical, measurable things like saving you time, saving you money, making you money, losing pounds, getting more visits to your website, and so on.

Intangible benefits are appealing values that are less physical and more difficult to measure. They include psychological and emotional things like greater peace of mind, increased confidence, and reduced stress.

Then there's the *benefit of taking action*, which is closely linked with *the benefit of the consequences of not taking action*. For instance, when I encourage people to create sales scripts, I let them know that the benefit of taking action by creating sales scripts is that they will close at a higher ratio, and thus make more money. The consequence of not taking action is that, for every presentation you deliver without having an effective sales script, you leave money on the table.

The last type of benefit is *the benefit of the benefit*. This is the indirect, often unstated or subconscious benefit linked to the direct benefit of a product. For instance, the direct benefit of my sales training is making more sales, but a benefit of that benefit might be achieving a better lifestyle where you can spend more time with your family. In many cases, the benefit of the benefit is the real reason why people buy.

Almost all products and services have multiple benefits. When writing your benefits script, the first and most essential step is to list all the benefits of your product or service that you can think of. You can then identify the top three to five benefits that will appeal most to your target market. You can further customize this for individual prospects by using your probing questions to identify the benefits that will most appeal to that particular prospect's "buyer fingerprint," Dr. Moine's term for the pattern that defines a person's buying criteria.

Exercise

Make a laundry list of all of the benefits of your product or service:

_____   _____

_____   _____

_____   _____

_____   _____

_____   _____

_____   _____

_____   _____

Writing Offer Scripts

Your close is the most crucial key to whether or not your presentation results in a sale, so your offer script is one of your most important scripts. If you have a weak presentation and a strong close, you can often still get sales. It is harder to get sales from a good presentation with a weak close.

The foundation of a good close is a strong offer. A strong offer is an offer where the reward represented by the benefits you offer outweighs the risk to the prospect. You can visualize this as a mental teeter-totter in your prospect's mind. On one side of the teeter-totter is price and other potential risks such as lost time. On the other side is value. Stacking as much value as you can on one side of the teeter-totter while reducing the risk as much as you can on the other side is the key to creating a good offer.

The components of your offer make up what goes on each side of the teeter-totter. This can include:

- Name of product or service
- Price
- Methods and terms of payment
- Benefits
- Features
- Specifications

- What's included
- What's not included

- Bonuses
- Length of contract
- Guarantee
- Warranty
- Incentive for buying today
- Risk of not buying today (scarcity)

- Call to action
- Order mechanism

Not all offers will include all of these components. Use this list to help you select the pieces that fit your offer.

The sequence of your closing offer includes three subsections:

- The *transition into the close*
- The *body of the close*
- The *final, final close*

In the *transition*, you move from the benefits section of your presentation into your close by using a connecting statement. Here are a few examples of transitional formulas:

- "What I would like to do now is share with you how I work with clients like you."
- "What I would like to do now is share how my ongoing coaching program works."
- "What I would like to do now is share with you the next step if you would like to work with me."

In the *body* of the close you explain your offer. Here you organize the list of the components of your offer into a sequence that explains them to the prospect. Arrange your sequence and choose your vocabulary so as to emphasize the components that are most important for you to highlight. For instance, if one of the features or bonuses that's included in your offer is more attractive than another feature, you might highlight the benefits of that item. Use your knowledge of your market and your prospect to emphasize the most compelling features of your offer.

The *final, final close* is your call to action, extending an invitation for your prospect to take some action in order to accept your offer. Here are some examples of common ways to word a final, final close:

- "Are you ready to get started?"
- "Sign here, please."
- "You can start with a one-month supply or a three-month supply. What works best for you?"
- "To order call…"
- "To order go to this website link:"
- "Click the 'buy' button to order."

In my Silver Protege sales training program I teach about a dozen different closing techniques. You can create offer scripts using any of these techniques. Some of the closing techniques you can build into your scripts include:

1. *Preframe*: Letting someone know earlier in the presentation that you're going to make an offer so they're expecting a close later, reducing the odds of them resisting you making a sales pitch.

2. *Trial close*: A variation of preframing where you get someone to agree early in the presentation that if you can meet certain conditions during your presentation they will agree to buy, for example: "If I can reduce your monthly payments and get you $10,000 in cash at close would you like to refinance your mortgage?"

3. *Ask*: Asking a simple question, in the same form you would use to ask an everyday question like, "Would you like to go to lunch?"

4. *"How do you feel?" close*: A variation on the ask close where you ask how the prospect feels about moving forward with the next step in the sales process, for example: "How do you feel about getting started today?"

5. *Assumption close*: Wording your close on the assumption that the sale has been made, for example by asking, "Which credit card would you like to use today?"

6. *Alternate of choice close*: Limiting the prospect's options to a set of choices that both assume a sale, such as, "We can do a 3 month or 4 month listing. What would work best for you?"

7. *Order form close*: Walking your prospect through filling out an order form, using simple direct commands worded as instructions, such as, "Put your name here," "Jot down your mailing address," or "Put your credit card here."

8. *Sympathy close*: Building on rapport and appealing to the benefit of helping others by wording the close as an appeal for help, for example: "It would really help me out if you could buy some cookies from my daughter for the Girl Scouts. Most people are buying five boxes. Could you buy at least two?"

9. *Contrast close*: Stressing the contrast between the price you're asking and the benefits you're offering, for example, advertising a $1,000,000 home for $775,000.

10. *Leverage close*: Emphasizing the negative consequences that come from not accepting the call to action, as when collection agencies point out the consequences if you don't pay or insurance salesmen stress the risk of not buying insurance.

11. *Scarcity close*: Stressing the risk of limited availability, as illustrated by TV ads for offers that are not available in stores or are available for a limited time only.

12. *Ask and be silent close*: Asking for commitment and remaining silent while you wait for the prospect's reply: "Would you like to buy some Girl Scout Cookies?"

In order to apply these techniques to write an offer script, you can follow a simple three-step formula:

1. Make a list of the components of your close

2. Put the components in a sequence to create an outline

3. Write a mini-script for each section of the outline

To illustrate the result of applying this formula, here are the components of the closing script I use when selling my Gold Protege program where I teach sales scripting:

I. Transition into the close

II. Body of the close

    A. Name of program

    B. What is included

    C. What you will learn

    D. Bonus

    E. Total value of the program

    F. Guarantee

    G. Price discount for taking action

III. Final, final close

You can adapt this formula to create any closing offer script you need to write.

Exercise

Write down your close word-for-word. Focus on completion, not perfection. Follow these steps:

1. List the components of your close
2. Put the components in sequence
3. Write a mini-script for each component

Writing Objection Scripts

For many sales representatives, objection handling is the most challenging part of the sales process, but it doesn't have to be when you apply script writing. Script writing lets you anticipate common objections, prepare persuasive replies, and practice your response until it flows smoothly and naturally.

Objections are what people who aren't in sales call "concerns," which is a better term to use when talking to prospects. Why do people object to sales representatives? There are a few common reasons:

- The prospect does not have a need or is not interested.
- The prospect does not have urgency to buy now.
- The prospect doesn't think they have the money or they truly don't have the money.
- The prospect is not the decision maker.
- The prospect does not want to change or they believe change will be too painful.
- The prospect thinks they can do it on their own or they don't need you.

These rationale for objections generate a few common objections that sales representatives in almost any industry meet:

- I need to think about it.
- I don't have any money.
- I need to talk it over with someone.
- Can you fax me some information?
- I don't have the time.
- Your price is too high.
- I am already working with someone.
- We already tried it and it didn't work.
- I'm not interested.

Any industry typically has some of these objections, plus a few variations of these and other objections specific to that industry. In any industry there tend to be about seven to twelve common objections.

The good news is that this means you can prepare persuasive responses for your industry's common objections. The strategy I teach is to first list your industry's common objections and then create responses for each objection. You can create effective responses by applying a few objection-handling tactics

I teach in my Silver Protege program. I teach over a dozen techniques to handle objections:

1. *Story*: Use a story about a client who had a similar objection but bought your product or service and got great results that met the objection.

2. *Non-stated*: Address the unstated assumption underlying the prospect's objection.

3. *Question*: Answer with a question, for instance, if they object, "The price is too high?", you can ask, "How much is too high?"

4. *Solve the problem*: Solve the problem that prompts the objection.

5. *Isolate the objection*: Ask questions to make sure the stated objection is the only objection so you can focus on answering it, such as responding to a money objection with the question, "Other than money, is there anything preventing you from moving forward?"

6. *Bring out the objection*: Ask questions to determine if there are any unstated objections underlying the stated objection.

7. *Investigative selling*: Investigate the reasons for the objection by responding, "Tell me more about that."

8. *Before it comes up*: Build a response to the objection into an earlier part of your presentation so that it does not come up in the closing phase of your presentation.

9. *Show the benefits*: Overcome the perception that your offer lacks a sufficiently strong value proposition by emphasizing the value of its benefits.

10. *Reduce the risk*: Add weight to the value side of your offer's teeter-totter by removing risks that counterbalance it.

11. *Be unreasonable*: Make an unreasonable request to force the prospect to justify their objection (not always applicable, but occasionally useful).

12. *Negotiate*: Adjust the offer to something the prospect finds reasonable by changing a term such as the price or another component of your close.

13. ***What would need to happen...?***: Get the prospect to visualize a scenario where they would accept your offer by asking what would need to happen in order for them to accept it.

14. ***Intuition***: After training in scripted objection-handling, you will develop the ability to use your intuition to handle unscripted objections.

I teach my students to use these objection-handling techniques to develop multiple responses to each of their industry's common objections. First, list your industry's common objections. Then write multiple responses to each objection. Set a goal of developing 10 to 20 responses to each common objection in your industry. Do this for each product or service you sell.

Here is an example of this method in action. In response to the objection sometimes encountered in the seminar industry, "I can't get off work to attend," here are five possible responses:

1. If you could get off work, would you attend?
2. Is that your only concern?
3. If you knew that by attending you could create so much cash that you could quit your job, would you attend?
4. Have you ever taken time off before?
5. Other than time, is there anything preventing you from moving forward?
6. Develop your own responses to the objections common in your industry.

Exercise

For one of the products or services you sell, list 7 to 12 objections you commonly encounter or might encounter. For each objection, script at least 3 responses by applying the techniques listed above.

Writing Other Parts of Your Scripts

Once you've completed your five laundry lists, you'll have many of the key pieces you need to complete scripts from other parts of your sales process outside the main body of your presentation. Here are a few tips on completing your lead generation, appointment booking, and follow-up sales scripts.

Lead Generation Scripts

In the chapter on script outlining I gave a script template I frequently use for lead generation talks, containing these components:

1. Intro
2. Outcomes
3. Chunk 1
4. Chunk 2
5. Chunk 3
6. Call to Action

The *Intro* section opens the presentation by building trust and rapport. I greet the audience and introduce myself and my topic by using stories and other techniques such as small talk and humor.

In the *Outcomes* section I give a preview of what points I'm going to cover, and what benefits the audience will get from those points. I also preframe my close by mentioning that I'll be making an offer at the end of the presentation. In a purely lead-generation talk, the offer is geared towards getting contact information rather than selling anything.

The *middle "Chunk" sections* cover the main content of the presentation. The key points are broken down into bite-sized "chunks" that can be easily digested, hence the name. Between each chunk I usually include a story to illustrate the point and keep the presentation dramatic.

The *Call to Action* is an offer script that uses the same approach covered above for that type of script. In a lead generation context, the offer focuses on offering something of value in exchange for contact information. However if you're going to sell something from the front of the room, you can use this same formula for that purpose as well.

This is just one example of a lead generation script, geared towards front-of-the-room presentations and their long-distance equivalents such as teleseminars and webinars. You can develop many other types of lead generation scripts for different contexts, such as networking events, email, and social media. In later chapters I'll give sample scripts for some of these different contexts.

Appointment Setting Scripts

You can also write scripts for appointment setting. An appointment-setting script contains the same basic ingredients as a sales presentation, but instead of selling a product or service, you're selling the appointment by demonstrating that the value of the appointment is worth the cost in the prospect's time.

This means that you must focus on conveying the standalone benefits of the appointment apart from any product or service you would be selling during the appointment. You must show that the appointment offers something of value to the prospect. So the place to start writing an appointment-setting script is by identifying the benefits of your appointment. Here are a few reasons why someone might want to meet with you:

- You're fun to talk to
- It's free to talk
- You have great ideas to share with them
- You can talk with them in the convenience of their home or office
- You can talk at a time that is convenient for them
- You will be giving them free bonuses for meeting with you
- You will answer their questions
- You will share how the benefits of your product or service can help them
- You will give them a no-risk opportunity to move forward if they are comfortable and if not, no problem

After identifying the benefits of meeting with you, you can work these benefits into the structure of an appointment setting script. The sequence I use for writing an appointment setting script generally follows this template:

1. Greeting identifying who I am
2. Explaining the reason for the conversation
3. Explaining what I'd like to do during the appointment
4. Asking the prospect if they'd like to meet

To apply this template, I use language such as this:

1. Hello, this is … I'm calling for … Is this … ?
2. The reason I'm calling is …
3. What I'd like to do is … How it works is …
4. How do you feel about scheduling an appointment? … I am open on … What works best for you? Would you like to schedule an appointment?

This version of the script is geared towards phone calls. You can adapt the same template to other formats such as face-to-face meetings, email conversations, and social media conversations.

Follow-up Scripts

One other section of your sales presentation you can script is your follow-up. The real fortune in sales is in the follow-up. One reason many sales representatives aren't more successful is that they give up if they don't close a sale after the first meeting. But studies show that most sales aren't closed until six to twelve or more contacts with a prospect, and in a social media context it often takes many more contacts.

One element of your follow-up to script is what you will do and say if your first meeting with a prospect does not result in either a sale or a firm, "No." Will you call back in a day? Send them an email? Mail them a letter? Decide on your follow-up model and then write a script to support it.

Another aspect of your follow-up you can script is offering **upsell**, **downsell**, or **cross-sell** opportunities.

An **upsell** is when you offer a more expensive product or service than the one you initially offered or sold. For instance, I normally offer graduates of my Silver Protege program my Gold Protege program. However, I sometimes encounter experienced sales representatives who are not interested in the Silver Protege program but are in the market for the Gold Protege program, in which case I may offer this to them instead of Silver.

A **downsell** uses the opposite strategy, offering a less expensive product or service. An example would be if you had an expensive live event someone could not afford to attend, so you offered them a less expensive DVD covering a recording of part of the event.

A **cross-sell** is when you offer a related product or service. For instance, I often let prospects and customers on my mailing list who have expressed interest in one of my programs know about programs offered by my JV partners.

You can write follow-up scripts for upsell, downsell, or cross-sell offers. Plan the sequence of how your offer will follow up on your initial sales contact. Then write the script to support that sequence.

A third type of follow-up script you can write is an email **autoresponder** sequence. An autoresponder sequence is a series of emails you use a software program to send automatically at set intervals after someone has signed up for your mailing list. For instance, you might create a sequence that sends someone an email once a day for five business days after they register to download a free report from your website.

Exercise

Review your follow-up procedures. Identify any procedures you use that need scripts. Outline and write your follow-up scripts.

Ideas Into Action

Let me share a story with you about one of my star clients, Mandy Pratt, who made a decision to master these skills. She was delivering a sales presentation over the phone selling a high-priced, wealth-building program. The program was around $6,000. Here's how the dance with the prospect went:

Mandy: "How do you feel about moving forward?"

Prospect: "I don't have the money."

Mandy: "Other than the money, is there anything else that's preventing you from moving forward?"

Prospect: "Well, it's actually not the money. It's my husband."

Mandy: "Tell me more about that."

Prospect: "Well, I bought a program similar to this a few years ago without first talking it over with my husband. The program didn't work and we were out several thousands dollars, and my husband was very upset with me. I'm concerned that if I buy this program tonight, my husband might be unhappy with me."

Mandy: "I understand. So you want to find out how your husband feels about this before you make an investment in the program?"

Prospect: "Exactly."

Mandy: "Let me ask you a question—is your husband home tonight?"

Prospect: "Yes."

Mandy: "Let's put him on the line and I will share with him that you have an interest in the program and that you want to hear if he has any concerns before moving forward. How does that sound?"

Prospect: "I can do that."

[The woman's husband joined the conversation.]

Mandy: "Sir, I was talking with your wife who is very interested in one of our programs. This is what the program is. It costs $6,000. She said that you both had a bad experience before and she don't want to do anything without you first knowing what she was doing and secondly, that you felt that that was a good decision. We wanted to know how you feel about this?"

After talking for a few more minutes, the husband said, "Listen, if this is what my wife wants to do, she has my blessing." Mandy made a $6,000 sale. Her commission was 20 percent, which meant that she earned a $1,200 commission on that single sale. More importantly, Mandy has the skill set to "elegantly dance with the prospect." She is currently in her thirties and she will have that skill set for the rest of her life, making her hundreds of thousands of dollars in increased commissions.

Key Points Review

- Work on your scripts section by section.

- To get started, motivate yourself by visualizing the financial and lifestyle benefits of having your scripts completed; focus on completion instead of perfection; and start with your baseline script or a borrowed script.

- Work on your five laundry lists first.

- Use your five laundry lists to help you complete other parts of your scripts.

Chapter 9

Persuasion Engineer
Your Script

Automotive engineers apply science to vehicle design in order to improve factors such as fuel efficiency, speed, and safety. NLP psychology practitioners Richard Bandler and John La Valle borrowed the engineering metaphor to introduce the idea of using the science of psychology to engineer the persuasiveness of sales presentations, calling this "persuasion engineering." I learned persuasion engineering from Dr. Donald Moine, who is the world's leading expert in NLP sales applications. I teach a simple three-step approach to persuasion engineering that you can use even if you don't know NLP. After you finish writing a complete first draft of the sections of your script, the next step is to persuasion engineer it.

The Persuasion Engineering Process

The persuasion engineering process involves a three-step review of your script and its component mini-scripts. Review each section of your script checking each of the following areas:

1. Sequence: Is this in the best order?
2. Inclusion: Is this item needed?
3. Persuasiveness: Is this the most persuasive way for me to say this?

Let's break these three steps down.

Sequence

Sales Mountain represents the optimal sales sequence of a generic sales presentation. Each mini-script section of your script also has its own customized, optimal sales sequence. You can improve the persuasiveness of your script by improving the flow of your script's sequence.

When reviewing your script's sequence, you can consider a number of items:

- Does my overall script follow the Sales Mountain sequence?
- Do I have a good introductory sequence to break the ice?
- Do I include transitions between key sections? Do I ask permission before introducing my probing questions? Do I transition into the close?
- Does each section have a clear beginning and conclusion?
- Are the items in each subsection arranged in a sequence that highlights the most important items? Are my most important probing questions first? Are my most important benefits first? Does my close highlight the most compelling values? Have I covered the objections that are most likely to come up?
- Does the timing of my sequence transitions give me enough time to get my close in during the allotted time?
- For instance, if I've promised a prospect a 30-minute free coaching session, am I starting my close in time to deliver it before the 30 minutes expires?

Review the sequence of your script and mini-scripts using these criteria as a checklist.

Inclusion

The next step is to review what your script includes to see if there are any items that can be removed to streamline your presentation. Just as a sculptor hacks away at extra material to reveal the form beneath, or just as a film editor edits out extra takes to produce a final cut, you can bring out the best in your script by removing extra items that dilute the power of your presentation. Check to see if there are any items that don't serve a purpose or detract from the impact of your most essential items. Ask yourself questions such as:

- Are there any stories that won't interest my audience, that go on too long, or that might offend them?
- Are there any questions on my list of probing questions that aren't relevant to what my prospect might need or what I need to know?
- Are there any items on my list of benefits that won't help sell my offer?
- Is there anything in my close I don't need to mention to sell my offer?
- Are any of my objection responses irrelevant or unlikely to come up?

Use these types of questions to prune your scripts and mini-scripts of unnecessary elements and trim them down to the essentials.

Persuasiveness

A third step is reviewing your presentation's overall persuasiveness. Here you check to see if the language and flow of thought you are presenting is compelling enough to motivate your prospect to take action on your offer. To evaluate this, there are a number of items you can review to make your presentation more compelling:

- Is this the most persuasive way for me to say this?
- Is this the strongest emotional vocabulary I could use?
- Are these the most vivid sensory images I could use?
- Are these the clearest descriptions I could use?
- Are these the strongest call-to-action verbs I could use?
- Do my points follow a comprehensible sequence?
- Do my arguments make logical sense?
- Does the action I want my prospect to take follow from the value I have presented?

Use these types of questions to help you review the persuasiveness of your presentation and identify places you can improve.

Exercise

Take one of your completed scripts and persuasion engineer it. Review it for:

1. Optimal sequence
2. Inclusion of unnecessary items
3. Persuasiveness of overall presentation

Ideas into Action

Shay Brown works for a training company that does customer service and sales training. Around 2006, he was doing $80,000 a year at his business but was still strapped financially. I taught him how to use a script to get himself booked for free speeches for sales training and how to script out the speech to sell sales training products. Shay has done that for last nine years. One script has brought in over $4 million. He has conservatively done additional $1 million by applying my sales scripting methods. Today Shay no longer feels financial pressure and is excited about the future. He is only in his 40s and he has these sales skills to earn him money for the rest of his life.

Key Points Review

- Persuasion engineer your scripts to make them more compelling.
- Review the sequence of your script and its subscripts to make sure they are in optimal order.
- Review what your script includes to identify any items you can remove to streamline your script.
- Review the persuasiveness of your script by optimizing the selection of your language and the presentation of your flow of thought.

Chapter 10

Revise, Improve, and Update Your Script

I was working with one of my coaches once and he introduced me to a great probing question: "Do you know exactly what to say to get someone to buy from you?" When I heard this, I realized it would be a great probing question to use in my presentations. I borrowed it and added it to my probing question scripts.

This is an example of the final step in the sales scriptwriting process: revising, improving and updating your script. In this step, after you've started using the script you completed in the last step, you continue looking for ways to make your script better. You can do this in three ways: revising, improving, and updating.

Revise

The word "revise" comes from a Latin phrase meaning "to look at again." In English this carries the connotation of looking at something again in light of new information with an eye towards making improvements. For instance, a revised edition of a textbook might include references to new discoveries that have been made since the original edition was published, as well as corrections to errors noticed by readers. Just as you can revise a book after publishing it, you can revise a script you've started using in light of feedback you get from using the script during your sales presentations.

There are a few sources of feedback you should pay attention to when revising your scripts. These include self-review, feedback from your audience, and analysis of your sales numbers.

Self-review

First, there is the internal feedback you get from the thoughts and feelings you experience while delivering the script. Get in the habit of debriefing yourself after you've delivered a sales presentation to check your performance. Create a checklist of self-review questions, like this:

- How did the script sound to you when you said it out loud?
- What parts felt emotionally compelling and logically persuasive, where you felt like you were delivering a powerful presentation?
- Were there any parts that felt weaker than others, where you felt more hesitant in your delivery?
- Did your stories sound interesting?
- Did you ask the right probing questions to identify your prospect's needs?
- Did you convey the benefits you needed to highlight effectively?
- Did your close make a strong offer?
- Did you handle objections effectively?

Using this type of checklist as a guideline, walk through each section of your script reviewing where your delivery felt strong and where it could be strengthened.

Audience Feedback

A second source of feedback comes from the audience of your presentation. In some cases this will be an individual or a series of individuals, in other cases it might be a group. In either case, there are several things you should pay attention to:

First, pay attention to **what your audience says** in response to your presentation. If possible, record your presentation so you have a record of their exact words. Otherwise, write down any important notes as soon as you get a chance so you don't forget.

Second, notice any important *nonverbal feedback*. Most communication is nonverbal. Make eye contact with your audience so you can pay attention to visual cues such as eye movements, facial expressions, posture, and gestures. Listen for auditory cues such as tone of voice changes or laughter during stories. For instance, stand-up comedians test jokes with different audiences to see which ones get the best laughs, which is a technique you can adopt when telling humorous stories.

Third, notice *what your audience does* in reaction to your presentation. Actions speak louder than words. For instance, if the purpose of a lead generation talk was to get people to fill out contact information forms and no one filled out a form when you were done with your presentation, something went wrong, and you need to review what happened to look for possible causes. Was it something you said? Were the directions unclear? Were the forms too hard to fill out? Did someone forget to pass the forms out at the right time? Similarly, notice what follow-up actions your audience takes after you leave a voicemail, book an appointment, deliver a close, or take other actions that prompt an audience response.

Get in the habit of paying attention to the feedback your audience gives you through their words, body language, and actions in response to your script. Record your results and review them so you can make adjustments.

Sales Numbers

A third, vitally important source of feedback is your sales numbers. Your numbers provide you with the most objective measurement of the effectiveness of your scripts. Pay attention to key numbers associated with your sales scripts, such as:

- Which scripts generate the most leads?
- Which scripts generate the most appointments?
- Which scripts generate the most sales?
- Which stories am I using in the scripts that get the best results?
- Which probing questions am I using in my best-performing scripts?
- Which benefits am I stressing in my best-closing scripts?

- Which of my closing scripts generates the most sales?
- Which objections come up most frequently in my presentations, and which answers am I using when I'm closing the most sales?

Using these types of questions to track your sales numbers is one of the most effective ways to boost your sales scripts' performance.

An advanced application of this strategy used in copywriting and advertising is called "A/B testing" or "split testing." In split testing, you test an A version and a B version of an ad with one variable changed and compare the results. For instance, you might keep everything in the ad the same but change the headline. You test the different versions of the ad out on a large number of consumers to see which version performs better statistically.

You can apply the split testing method to your scripts as well by trying out different versions of your script. Ideally, the best way to do this is to keep everything in the two versions the same and only change the one variable you're trying to test at a given time. It's also a best practice to conduct your test on a sufficiently large number of people or cases. In statistics, the larger your sample size, the more reliably you can interpret your results. Because of this, most national polls collect at least 1,000 responses. Direct mail marketers, Internet marketers, and radio and TV advertisers may test on scales of thousands, tens of thousands, or even more.

However, in many practical situations, you may not have the resources available to do a large-scale split test. In this case, just do your best to test your scripts on whatever scale you can. You can gather a lot of valuable feedback by simply testing different versions of scripts on individual audiences and monitoring their reactions.

Combine the information you get from your sales numbers with the feedback you get from your audiences and your own self-observations to help you revise your scripts.

Improve

The purpose of revising your scripts is to adjust areas that need improvement. There are three basic ways to improve any script: *changing* the existing script, *adding* pieces, and *deleting* pieces. To illustrate each of these script editing techniques, I'm going to use examples from the script of one of my favorite movie series, *Star Wars*. The first *Star Wars* movie, later subtitled *Episode IV: A New*

Hope, was originally released in 1977. It was edited for re-release in theaters in 1997, then edited again for DVD in 2004 and Blu-ray in 2011.

Changing

When George Lucas originally produced *Star Wars* in 1977, his ability to bring his vision to life was limited by the technology of the time, as well as by time and budget constraints. He improved existing special effects techniques and experimented with new ones, and took the industry to a new level, but the results still did not fully satisfy him. After his special effects company Industrial Light & Magic produced the special effects for Steven Spielberg's 1993 movie *Jurassic Park*, Lucas concluded that digital technology was now capable of bringing his vision more fully to life.

For the 1997 Special Edition release celebrating the film's 20th anniversary, Lucas used digital special effects to change a number of scenes in the original movie. For instance, when the Stormtroopers begin searching for the Droids in the desert of Tatooine, they are mounted on dinosaur-like creatures called dewbacks. In the original film, there was a single life-sized dewback puppet. The puppet had limited movement capability, so it was kept stationary in the background of the scene. But Lucas had always envisioned the dewback moving and was never satisfied with the scene. In the 1997 re-release, computer animation was used to replace the puppet dewback with several digital dewbacks moving in both the background and the foreground of the shot over some new live footage of additional Stormtroopers. The process used to achieve this change is documented in a short video called "Anatomy of a Dewback" which you can watch on starwars.com.

As you deploy your sales scripts, you might find there are pieces you're not satisfied with that can be improved by changing them. For instance, you might decide to change the story you use to illustrate a point. You might change one of your probing questions. You might change which benefit you stress first. You might change the price in your close. You might change how you handle a certain objection.

Adding

The 1997 version of *Star Wars* also added some scenes to the original film. For instance, when filming the 1977 production, Lucas originally shot several scenes where Luke Skywalker talks to his childhood friend Biggs Darklighter, who joins the Rebellion before Luke. Most of these scenes were cut from the final film, and we only catch a brief hint at Luke and Biggs' prior relationship during the film's final scene at the Battle of Yavin, just before Biggs dies in combat protecting Luke from Darth Vader's TIE Fighter. In the 1997 re-release, a scene of Biggs and Luke meeting on the planet Yavin before the battle has been added back in, adding meaning to Biggs' later death scene.

You can add new elements to your scripts to improve them. You can introduce new stories, more probing questions, extra benefits, new closing components, or different answers to objections.

Deleting

Several scenes that were shot for the original 1977 *Star Wars* were deleted from the final film for reasons such as time, narrative pacing, special effects, or other editorial considerations. For instance, in one deleted scene from the beginning of the film, Luke is supposed to be working on his uncle's farm when he looks at the sky through his binoculars and sees a space battle. The battle turns out to involve the Rebel blockade runner carrying the Droids and the stolen plans for the Death Star. Luke runs and tells his friends, which leads to a conversation with Biggs about the Rebellion. Lucas added this scene after friends previewing the script told him they thought the story took too long to introduce Luke. But after filming the scene, Lucas had second thoughts about how the extra scene slowed the pace of the film down, and he decided to edit it out of the theatrical release. This scene has never been officially restored to the film, though it was included in a 1998 CD-ROM release called *Star Wars: Behind the Magic*, and it also appeared in early children's book, novel, and comic-book adaptations of the film.

When you're editing your script, you may decide that some parts need to be deleted. Maybe one of your stories doesn't land the point you're trying to get across. Maybe one of your probing questions is asking for unnecessary information. Maybe one of the benefits you mention isn't a strong selling point. Maybe your close includes details you don't need to highlight at that point in your presentation. Maybe you're addressing an objection that doesn't need to come up if you use a different approach earlier in your presentation. Sometimes what you leave out of your presentation can have as much impact as what you leave in.

Update

Sometimes your script needs to be updated to incorporate new information. Going back to the example of *Star Wars*, when the original film came out, the title was simply *Star Wars*. After the first sequel *The Empire Strikes Back* came out and the original film was re-released, its opening sequence added the sub-title *Episode IV: A New Hope* to reflect the fact that it was now part of a series. Later re-releases of the next sequel, *Return of the Jedi*, added a new closing sequence tying the film into the prequels that now form Episodes I through III of the series.

Similarly, you will sometimes need to update your sales scripts. For example, as I train more sales students, I am constantly collecting new success stories to add to my story file. You might also need to update your scripts to reflect developments such as a change in price, a new market you're trying to penetrate, a new application or benefit you've discovered, a new objection you've been encountering recently, or the release of a new product or service line. Keep your scripts up-to-date to reflect your current situation.

When you update your scripts, it's a best practice to save them as new files and keep your files of your original scripts. You may find it useful to have your original scripts available so you can document and review which changes you made. You can keep track of which file is most current by adding an identifying number to the end of the file name, such as a date.

Exercise

Review the scripts you've been using. Identify any areas that can be revised, improved, or updated.

Ideas Into Action

Robert Fox's company serves an area of the business process outsourcing business called business processing services, providing virtual assistant, contact center, and website and mobile app development services. His company uses sales scripts for applications such as helping clients develop social media, telemarketing, and call center scripts. Robert had 20 years of sales training before meeting me, but he says I was the first person who ever gave him complete instructions on how to write a successful sales script, which has increased his results dramatically. He estimates that my scripting techniques have generated thousands of dollars for his own company and millions for their clients. Robert writes, "A 5% shift in a script can have a 500% shift in results, it's not just the words and how there said and the meaning that they carry with them. . . One of the most important things that I've gained from working with [Eric] is a better understanding of when you're writing a good script. Simple scripts can often be the best, they're quick rebuttals and very effective and that's the one thing that I've learned the most from [Eric]. Many other sales professionals teach very long rebuttals that quite frankly are difficult to get out and often times can lead your prospect astray. Short one-word answers can be very poignant and effective. . . There are very few people that teach professional sales training with a high ethical standard. Eric Lofholm happens to be one of those people."

Key Points Review

- ■ You can make your scripts better by revising, improving, or updating them.

- ■ To revise your scripts, review them in light of feedback you get from your own self-review of your presentations, from your audience's reactions, and from your sales numbers.

- ■ Improve your scripts by changing, adding, or deleting elements.

- ■ Update your scripts to reflect the latest changes to your sales situation.

Chapter 11

Types of Scripts

In the film and television industry, there are many different types of scripts for different genres. There's drama, comedy, action, romance, mystery, thriller, science fiction, fantasy, horror, and more. Each of these genres has various subgenres. For instance, within the comedy genre there is the physical comedy style represented by slapstick masters like Buster Keaton, the Three Stooges, Lucille Ball, Jerry Lewis, John Ritter, Jim Carrey, and Jackie Chan. There are pun-oriented comedies like the film and TV work of Groucho Marx, Abbot and Costello's "Who's on first?" skit, and the "What's our vector, Victor?" scene from the movie *Airplane*. There is the satirical comedy style illustrated by *Saturday Night Live*, *The Simpsons*, and *South Park*. Each of these genres can be delivered through different media, with *The Simpsons* and *South Park* showing how comedy styles can be adapted to TV animation.

There are many different types of sales scripts as well. Different types of scripts are designed for different phases of the sales process and different communications settings and media. In this chapter we'll take a look at types of scripts designed for face-to-face presentations; front-of-the-room talks; phone calls; email; social media; textual formats such as blogs, articles, and books; and multimedia contexts such as audio and video.

I'll focus on pulling together distinctions we've already covered in previous chapters, with an emphasis on how to structure the various types of sales scripts, along with general tips. Future chapters will provide more specific samples of different types of sales scripts.

Face-to-face Presentations

Scripts for face-to-face sales presentations form the foundation for other types of sales scripts. Face-to-face selling is the most natural and common form of selling. If you master the principles of scripting face-to-face selling, you have a solid foundation for adapting sales scripts to other contexts. For this reason, I'll place the emphasis in this chapter on face-to-face scripts to teach you some distinctions you can apply to other types of scripts. Pay close attention to this section even if you plan to focus on other types of scripts, because much of what I say here also applies to other scripting categories.

Foundation: Lead Generation

Before you can run a face-to-face sales presentation, you typically need to lay a foundation with a lead generation script. (There are exceptions, such as when Girl Scouts sell cookies door-to-door without prior contact.) Lead generation scripts can take many forms, including several of the other scripts covered in this chapter. For instance, you might use an elevator pitch, a speech, a webinar, or a phone call as a launching pad to book a sales presentation opportunity.

Whichever form of lead generation script you use, the main purpose of your script is to get prospects into your database in order to create an opportunity for booking an appointment to run a sales presentation. Design your script with this purpose in mind. Write a close that gives prospects an incentive for providing you with contact information. Gear the rest of your script towards building up to your close.

The structure of a lead generation script is similar to the structure of a sales presentation. As with a sales presentation, you lead with trust and rapport, progress through needs and benefits, and conclude with a close. The difference is that instead of selling a product or service in your close, you're selling the benefits of your prospect providing you with their contact information. The needs and benefits sections of your presentation should demonstrate to them that providing you with their contact information will help address their needs and deliver them value. For instance, one way to do this is to address one to three of the most common problems faced by your target market and offer actionable tips on each topic. This demonstrates that your expertise can help your prospects with their needs, giving them an incentive to want follow-up contact with you.

The offer in your lead generation close can take a number of forms depending on your sales model and what medium you're using. For instance, you might offer an opportunity to book a free consultation, sign up for a mailing list to get free information, or request a free book, audio, or video.

When it comes to objection handling in lead generation scripts, your best strategy is to pre-empt possible objections by building responses into your presentation. Identify the most common objections in your industry, and use the objection-handling techniques described in other chapters to answer these objections before they come up.

Another important objection-handling strategy for lead generation scripts is to reduce the risk for prospects providing you with contact information. Reduce the effort involved by providing an easy response mechanism, such as a physical form that prospects can fill out or that you can fill out form them, a QR code they can scan with their smartphone, a social media button they can click, a webinar registration form they can enter, or an email opt-in form they can submit. For emails, reduce their risk by including a disclaimer ensuring them that you will not misuse their contact information to spam them or share their information with third parties.

Lead generation scripts should include follow-up scripts. Getting someone into your database is only the first step, and you will usually not get an appointment booked after only one contact. You may need to make several or even dozens of "touches" with your prospect before you succeed in booking an appointment. A touch is a follow-up contact though any medium, including face-to-face contact, phone calls, email, and social media. Increase your ability to make follow-up touches by designing your lead generation script to get your prospects onto some type of phone call list, mailing list, or social media list. To avoid being pushy, ask permission to engage in this type of follow-up contact. Your close should include language requesting this type of permission and offering value in exchange for granting such permission. For instance, you might ask someone if it's okay to call them to schedule a free consultation, emphasizing the value they will get out of it. Similarly, you might get website visitors to give you permission to email them by offering a free download of information in exchange for subscribing to your mailing list. Your follow-up emails should then include reminders that they are receiving your email by request and that they have the opportunity to opt out of your list at any time.

Setting the Stage: Appointment Booking

Appointment booking scripts are designed to convert the leads you have added to your database into sales appointments. Your script's main goal is to book an appointment where you deliver a sales presentation. This means that you shouldn't try to deliver your presentation during your appointment-booking script: save that for the appointment itself. I sum this distinction up by teaching my students, "The purpose of booking an appointment is to book an appointment."

With this purpose in mind, the close of your appointment-booking script should be designed to sell the prospect on the value of booking an appointment with you. You are asking them for their valuable time. What can you offer them in exchange? Depending on your business model, one option that works well is to offer a free initial consultation. This gives you an opportunity to connect with your prospect, listen to their needs, and demonstrate that you have solutions that meet their needs. Other options are to offer some type of free information, free membership, or another free gift or discount. Adapt the formula to your business model.

Your close should also reduce your prospect's risk. To ensure them that you will not waste their time, keep initial meetings limited in length. An initial consultation should usually run no more than a half hour to an hour. For cold call appointment-booking scripts, you should ask for even less of your prospect's time, in the range of five to fifteen minutes. Be sure to mention that the meeting is free. Similarly, if you are giving away a free infoproduct, keep it short and to the point, and emphasize that it is free with no obligation. For instance, if you are using a video to help book an appointment, keep the video short, ideally no more than three to ten minutes in length.

Another important risk-reducing technique is letting your prospect know up front if you will be offering them something. People don't like to be surprised by an unexpected sales pitch when they were expecting something free. To avoid generating a negative reaction, if you intend to make an offer at the end of an initial free consultation, make sure you include language in your appointment-booking script that signals your intent in a non-threatening way. For instance, you might mention that during the consultation you will be presenting them with some free tips and answering any questions they might have, and if it makes sense based on how the discussion goes, you will be offering them an opportunity to continue the discussion. This reduces the risk of making your prospect feel ambushed by a sales pitch they weren't expecting.

The heart of your close is inviting your prospect to schedule an appointment. The language of your script should be geared towards getting them to commit to a specific time and place or medium. Depending on the medium you will be using for your presentation, this might take the form of scheduling a face-to-face meeting with them, scheduling a phone call, or getting them to click on a link for an email list, social media list, video, or webinar.

In some cases, you might automate your appointment-booking process by using software. For instance, some of my sales trainers book their appointments using TimeTrade, an online appointment scheduling tool that lets prospects view an online calendar and fill out a digital form to schedule an appointment and receive a follow-up email confirmation and reminder.

Design the body of your appointment-booking script to support your close. After leading with trust and rapport, ask questions to identify what needs your prospect has that meeting with you might serve. Communicate how meeting with you will benefit your prospect. Pre-empt objections by stressing that you will respect their time and that there is no cost or obligation incurred by meeting with you.

Follow-up is an important part of the appointment booking process. Make it easy for your prospects to schedule an appointment with you. When appropriate, confirm the appointment and remind them of your meeting time using tools such as phone calls or email.

When scheduling a presentation that will be hosted by another party, it's a good practice to schedule a meeting with the host prior to the actual presentation. Following sales industry jargon I learned while working for Tony Robbins, I call this warm-up meeting the "boss talk" because it often involves meeting with the person in charge of running an event where you will be delivering your presentation. Although a boss talk is most typical in group presentation situations, a similar principle might also apply to one-on-one meetings which have been arranged by a referral partner who you want to consult prior to the meeting in order to help you feel out the prospect or warm them up. I'll say more about how the boss talk distinction applies in a front-of-the-room speech situation a little later in this chapter, but in a one-on-one or small group context arranged by a referral partner or another associate, consider meeting with your partner prior to your sales presentation to get their input on your prospect's needs and concerns.

Running the Presentation

Successfully scheduling an appointment gives you the opportunity to deliver your sales presentation script. Your script will follow the Sales Mountain sequence outlined in earlier chapters of this book. In previous chapters I shared some specific techniques for scripting each step in the sequence. Here I will focus on pulling these pieces together into the big picture of your overall presentation script.

Building trust and rapport lays the foundation for successful delivery of your script. Here I've emphasized the importance of scripting stories to help you connect with your prospect. Your body language and how you greet your prospect are also important parts of building trust and rapport. Your facial expressions, gestures, posture, and tone of voice should be relaxed and friendly. The language you use to say hello and initiate the conversation should also create a friendly atmosphere, while simultaneously communicating professionalism. Small talk and jokes can help loosen up your prospect. Depending on your personality, you may find this comes to you naturally, or you may need to consciously practice how you greet people and develop specific scripts. Many public speakers collect jokes to help them warm up their audience, which is a practice sales representatives can borrow for presentations.

When moving into the probing questions section of your presentation, remember to include a transition so that you don't come across as aggressively interrogating your prospect like a cop grilling a suspect. One effective technique is asking your prospect if it's okay for you to ask them some questions in order to help you identify their needs so you can better assist them. Once they agree, you can then proceed with your probing questions. One effective way to deliver your probing questions is to ask your prospect to rate their needs in different areas on a scale of 1 to 10.

The most natural way to transition from your probing questions section into your benefits is to frame your benefits as solutions to the needs identified through your probing questions. For example, after running them through some questions where you ask them to rate their needs on a scale of 1 to 10, you might use their answers as a basis for providing them with three useful tips. This demonstrates the value you can deliver them.

After you've demonstrated enough value to deliver your close, it's important to transition into your close. One way to do this is to use a phrase such as, "What I'd like to do now is offer you an opportunity. . ." After using a variation of this formula, you can then proceed with the body of your close where you make your offer. Finally, conclude your close with your call to action. Your close is the heart of your presentation and the key to making a sale, so I recommend scripting your close word-for-word and rehearsing it until you can recite it smoothly.

After delivering your close, you will often need to use your objection handling scripts. Ideally, you should have pre-empted your industry's most common objections by building responses into earlier parts of your presentation and into your sales offer's price and terms. But even if you've done this, you may still need to answer some objections. Prepare yourself by scripting your responses and practicing them, as recommended in earlier chapters. When you practice, be sure to practice maintaining confident, non-defensive body language and voice tone as well. How you say things can be as important as what you say when handling objections.

Script and rehearse your follow up actions. For presentations where your close results in a sale, script how you will finalize the transaction and deliver the product or service. For presentations where the prospect does not buy immediately, script how you will follow up with additional touches. For presentations where the prospect says no, you might consider scripts asking them for referrals to others they know who might have a need for your product or service.

If you follow these steps and script each step of your presentation, your closing rate should increase dramatically. Prioritize scripting and rehearsing your close. Once you've got your close down, concentrate on improving your scripts and delivery for the remaining items on your laundry list. Improving your stories, probing questions, and objection responses can each help boost your closing rate.

Front-of-the-room Talks

With front-of-the-room talks, there are three main considerations: what you do before, during, and after your talk.

Before Your Presentation: The Boss Talk

Before giving a front-of-the-room talk, if your talk will be hosted by another party, the best practice is to schedule a boss talk. As mentioned earlier, a boss talk is a meeting with the event host that you book after booking the event but prior to running the event. During the boss talk, get clarity on key details such as whether you have permission to sell from the front of the room, how many people will be in attendance, what the audience will be like, what audiovisual equipment will be available, and any compensation split arrangements.

During Your Presentation: The $2 Million Formula

When it comes to delivering your presentation, I generally start my script by building on the formula I mentioned in Chapter 7 when I was illustrating how to outline a lead generation speech. I call this the $2 Million Formula:

    I. Intro

   II. Outcomes

  III. Chunk 1

  IV. Chunk 2

   V. Chunk 3

  VI. Call to action

The *Intro* section builds trust and rapport with the audience in the process of introducing you and your topic. A good way to do this is by telling a story related to one of the key points you want to make. The story can be about you or about somebody or something else your audience will find interesting.

The *Outcomes* section lets your audience know what you're going to tell them, what they're going to get out of it, and what action you'd like them to take as a result. The easiest way to communicate these points is to name your presentation, list the main points from your speech outline, list the main benefits you'd like your audience to get out of your presentation, and tell them the main actions you'd like them to take after your presentation. If you're going to be selling something at the end of your presentation, you can preframe this by mentioning it. For instance, you might say, "At the end of my presentation, I'll be sharing an opportunity for you to receive a free coaching session with me."

Each **Chunk** corresponds to one of the main points in your presentation. Each of your main points can be structured around a need your audience has, a benefit they're interested in, or an objection they have. I usually include a story to illustrate each of my main points before moving on to the next chunk in the presentation.

The **Call to Action** section tells my audience what actions you'd like them to take in response to your presentation. The primary action is typically to purchase whatever you're selling, so this is the place in your presentation to deliver your close. The call to action can also include practical applications of the information you've covered in your presentation. For instance, if I've told my audience how to use affirmations to build a mindset for successful selling, I might give them an assignment to start doing sales affirmations.

This outline assumes a front-of-the-room presentation in the range of 30 minutes to an hour in length. For shorter or longer presentation formats, I add or subtract chunks as needed. In some cases where an event runs multiple sessions or even several days, elements of this outline may be repeated more than once. For instance, each major session of the presentation might have its own introduction, outcomes, and call to action.

When scripting a front-of-the-room talk, it's important to incorporate the ordering mechanism you plan to use in your close. For instance, if you're going to be handing out sign-up forms, be sure to mention this in your script, and be sure to prepare the forms and bring them with you to your presentation.

After Your Presentation: Follow-up

It's also essential to include follow-up steps in your script. How will you process orders that result from your presentation? How will you follow up with attendees who don't buy immediately? Have you done anything to capture their contact information so you can follow up? When you follow up, what will you say? Will you follow up by phone, email, or some other medium?

Virtual Talks

Virtual talks include *teleconferences*, *webinars*, and *video conferences*, which are some of the most efficient ways to reach large audiences with today's technology. The same principles apply for teleconferences and webinars. The main difference is that teleconferences are delivered over the phone and are purely audio in format, whereas webinars and video conferences include online visual aids in combination with audio. Webinar and video conference services often include the option of teleconference delivery with audio only.

Virtual Lead Generation

You can invite audiences to a virtual talk using any of the lead generation strategies we have previously discussed. Because your audience will need to go online to register, you will usually get the best results from lead generation strategies where your audience is already connected to the Internet, such as email, social media, and blog invitations.

Virtual Appointment Setting

The appointment-setting component of your sales funnel typically involves an online registration form placed on a page on your website or blog. After receiving your lead generation invitation, your prospect visits your registration page and enters their contact information, including their email. They then get redirected to a confirmation page and receive a confirmation email. The confirmation page and email contain instructions on how to call or log into the event.

You can usually opt to send one or more follow-up email reminders closer to the time of your event. Doing this will help boost your attendance rate. If you have contact with your audience on social media, you might post a reminder there as well.

Running Virtual Presentations

Running a teleconference or webinar as an administrator requires using some administrative codes to control functions such as muting and unmuting your audience, sharing screen views, and recording your talk. The specifics of these administrative codes vary from one virtual event service provider to the next.

It's a good idea to practice learning how to use the codes for your specific provider by running a test event before trying to run a live call.

Apart from handling these administrative commands, running a virtual event is essentially similar to giving a front-of-the-room talk. The three-chunk front-of-the-room formula I gave you earlier works well for virtual events as well.

The main difference from a front-of-the-room talk is that with teleconferences and webinars you and your audience cannot see each other, so you must make up for the lack of body language. Some ways to do this are paying special attention to your tone of voice, giving your audience a chance to ask live audio questions, and getting live feedback from your audience via instant messaging and social media posts.

Virtual Follow-up

Because the registration process for live events includes collecting your attendees' email addresses, you have an opportunity to follow up on your event with email marketing. As a best practice, you should send out an email expressing a thank-you for attending. You can also offer follow-up bonuses and offers, such as a free recording or transcript of the event or a free coaching session for attendees.

Phone Calls

Phone call scripts are similar in principle to face-to-face scripts and other types of scripts, but there are special considerations due to the nature of the media. For one thing, phone calls are an intimate form of communication where you are often talking to someone in the privacy of their home or office, and you must be aware of the fact that you're entering their territory. This is especially true if you're cold-calling someone you don't know.

Phone Lead Generation

Phone calling lead generation begins by collecting phone numbers. In a cold-calling situation, you're collecting numbers of people you don't know that you've obtained from sources such as a directories, mailing lists, or opt-in forms. In "warmer" prospecting situations, you may be collecting phone numbers by meeting prospects at business conferences or interacting with them through email or social media.

Phone Appointment Setting

Some phone call scripts are designed to set appointments. You may be calling someone in order to schedule an opportunity to deliver them a sales presentation, which may in turn also be delivered over the phone or it may be delivered through another medium. You may also be calling to confirm the details of an appointment you've already agreed upon in a previous communication.

When setting or confirming an appointment over the phone, it's important to remember that the purpose of setting an appointment is to set an appointment. Focus the call on getting your prospect to agree to schedule a meeting. Sell them on the value of the meeting. Don't sell them on your product or service yet: that's what your meeting is for. All you're trying to do at this point is schedule the meeting.

In order to persuade the other party to agree to a meeting, it's important to follow a few guidelines. First, identify and introduce yourself in a way that speaks to their interest. For instance, if you've spoken to them before or you know someone in common who put you in touch with them, you might mention that. If they aren't familiar with you or your company at all, briefly identify yourself in a way that makes you relevant to their interests. For instance, you might describe your company as helping people in their industry with a specific job title.

Second, get to the point. Let them know briefly why you're calling, why it's relevant to their needs, and how it benefits them.

Third, extend a clear offer to schedule a meeting. For instance, if you're offering a free consultation or group presentation, script your close to extend that invitation. Describe briefly what the offer is, what it includes, what value they will get out of it, and how they can take advantage of the opportunity.

Fourth, reduce their risk by emphasizing that you value their time and you don't intend to waste their time either on this call or during any meeting you schedule. For instance, after introducing yourself, you might mention that you only need to talk to them on the phone less than five minutes to see if what you're offering is potentially of interest to them. Similarly, you might stress that meeting with you won't take more than a set amount of time, such as fifteen or thirty minutes, or you might emphasize that it's free.

Fifth, the person you're calling will sometimes request more information.

Be prepared for this possibility by having more information you can send them and a script for a follow-up call or email after they've received the information. For instance, you might send them a video link and then call them back in a day to see what they thought of the video.

Finally, be prepared for the fact you will sometimes end up talking to an answering machine or a secretary. You should prepare back-up scripts to handle these situations and support your main phone script.

Phone Presentations

Running a phone presentation is essentially similar to running other types of live presentations, with a few key differences. One difference is that you have to rely on your voice without the benefit of body language. Another point to bear in mind is that you may be talking to someone in the privacy of their home or office and interrupting their regular routine. This makes it especially important to respect their time, which is a third consideration.

For the structure of a phone presentation, you can often use a variation of the three-chunk formula for front-of-the-room presentations. For instance, you can use a half-hour three-chunk free consultation to deliver sample value and set the stage for offering a paid program. You can shorten this formula and focus on one main chunk if you need to keep a call shorter.

Phone Follow-up

Phone scripts will often require some type of follow-up either over the phone or through another medium. For instance, a successful sale may require follow-up order processing and delivery of a product or service. If your prospect does not buy immediately, you may need to follow up with additional phone calls, emails, or meetings. Plan your follow-up procedure and write scripts to support your follow-up system.

Email

Email marketing can serve to support many other sales formats discussed in this chapter. For instance, when someone registers for one of your virtual events and enters their contact information, you can follow up by emailing them. Similarly, you can collect email contact information from people who attend your lead generation talks, visit your website, or follow your social media posts.

In order to do email marketing effectively, you need effective email scripts. Email scripts follow the same general structure as other types of sales scripts, but the different nature of the medium requires some significant adjustments to the content.

Email Lead Generation

The key to email lead generation is what Internet marketers call an ***opt-in form***. This is an online form where a visitor "opts in" to your mailing list by entering their contact information and giving you permission to email them. Permission is required due to federal anti-spam regulations.

An opt-in-form can appear on any type of web page. It frequently appears on a special type of web page called a "***squeeze page***". A squeeze page is designed to "squeeze" the visitor's contact information out of them by limiting them to only two options: either to enter their information into an opt-in form or to leave the page. To support this purpose, a squeeze page has a simplified design with a minimum of navigation options, in order to focus the visitor's attention on the desired action of filling out the opt-in form.

In order to motivate readers to fill out an opt-in form, you need to offer them sufficient value to justify the effort it takes them to fill out the form. You must also convince them that it's worthwhile to join yet another mailing list and receive even more email in their inbox. In the process, you must also reduce the risk of them entering their contact information, which exposes them to potential spam.

To achieve this, you must create a strong offer with minimal risk. Internet marketers typically do this by offering some free information, a free product, or a free service such as an initial consultation as a reward for opting into your mailing list. To reduce risk, opt-in forms include language promising not to spam readers or share their email information with others.

Your email lead generation script is the script you use to extend your opt-in offer to your website visitor. The standard format typically includes several elements based on a copywriting formula called ***AIDA***, which stands for:

Attention

Interest

Desire

Action

The steps in AIDA correspond roughly to the steps in Sales Mountain, greatly simplified to fit the format:

The ***attention*** part of your opt-in script is designed to build trust and rapport and get the visitor's attention in the process. This is usually achieved through an arresting headline, eye-catching graphic or video elements, and credibility builders such as testimonial quotes. For example, you might offer a free report with a title like "The Three Biggest Mistakes Small Business Owners Make" and use this to generate as a headline such as, "Avoid the #1 Mistake That Kills Most Small Businesses within 18 Months".

The ***interest*** component of your script speaks to your visitor's interests and needs, corresponding to probing questions. To appeal to your visitor's interest, use language and imagery that lets your visitor know your opt-in offer addresses their needs. For instance, building on our example, you might follow up your headline with text or a video describing some of the most common headaches small business owners experience.

The ***desire*** part of your script appeals to your visitor's emotions, corresponding to benefits. Here you offer a solution to the problem you introduced earlier. Continuing our example, you might introduce your free report as a way to avoid the small business headaches you described and experience entrepreneurial success.

The ***action*** conclusion to your script, also known as the ***call to action***, is where you extend your offer. Here you offer your reader something of value in exchange for entering their contact information. In our example, the value would be the free report.

The action portion of your script also includes instructions on how to take advantage of your offer. This typically includes brief instructions on how to fill in your opt-in form and submit it by clicking a button.

The purpose of using this type of opt-in script is to get your visitor to submit their contact information so you can enter them into your mailing list database. This enables you to follow up with additional email marketing efforts.

Email Appointment Setting

You can use emails to set appointments. In some cases, you might be emailing someone who has previously opted into your mailing list. In other cases, you might be emailing a new prospect you've met through some other means such as networking or social media.

When setting an appointment via email, the same general principles apply as when setting an appointment over the phone. Focus on scheduling an appointment, not trying to make a sale. Introduce yourself in a way that speaks to their interests. Be brief. Offer them value to make them want an appointment with you. Assure them that you value their time and don't intend to waste it.

Adapt these principles to the email format using the AIDA formula mentioned above. The attention-getting components of your email include your header information such as your name, your recipient's name, and your subject line, along with the opening of the body of your email. The rest of the body of your email should speak to your reader's interests, arouse their desire to schedule a meeting with you, and invite them to take action by scheduling a meeting.

As with phone calls, you may need to follow up by sending more information, such as a link to supporting sales material. You may also need to follow up with additional communication such as additional emails, phone calls, or a face-to-face visit.

Email Presentations

You can deliver a sales presentation by email. Generally, people do not buy from someone who emails them without prior communication, so a sales email usually comes after a series of prior contacts through email or other formats such as social media. Many Internet marketers find sales emails most effective if they are delivered after a series of prior emails providing free information or other value such as links to videos, blog posts, and resources.

The structure of a sales email follows the same AIDA format we have been discussing. The subject line must be carefully crafted to get the reader's attention and make them want to open the email. A P.S. line is often used as a second subject line to reinforce the main message and call to action of the email.

It is difficult to arouse interest and desire in a short email if you don't have a prior relationship with your prospect. For this reason, many Internet marketers prefer to support short sales emails with longer sales pitches delivered outside the email itself. This can be done through a series of prior emails or by using the email to direct the reader to a link to a longer sales page, a video, or another format where you can deliver more sales information. If you use this approach, you can keep the email itself short and focus it on getting the reader to click on a link to your longer, supporting sales piece.

Alternately, you can sell from the email itself by writing a longer email in the style of a direct mail piece. Copywriters with direct mail experience have found success using this approach.

Email Follow-up

Since most people do not buy the first time you send them a sales email, an effective email marketing strategy needs to include a follow-up strategy and scripts. Be prepared to email your prospect on an ongoing basis. This should generally include a number of non-sales emails providing valuable information, along with periodic sales emails. Dozens of non-sales emails are typically needed to build trust and rapport. For any given sales offer, you may need to send out more than one email. Many Internet marketers use a four-email formula spaced out over several days to promote major sales campaigns.

You can also integrate your email follow-up with other follow-up systems. For instance, you might create a system where you follow up a specific email with a phone call.

To automate your email follow-up procedure, you can use an email service called an *autoresponder*. An autoresponder service lets you automatically send someone who opts into your mailing list a series of prewritten emails spaced out over set intervals you choose. You can also use an autoresponder service to send out periodic newsletters and one-time special announcements.

Most autoresponder services let you *segment* your mailing list so that you can send specific emails to select subgroups from your mailing list who meet certain criteria. For instance, you can send an email to everyone on your list who previously opted into a specific offer or bought a specific product. This segmenting feature lets you focus your email marketing efforts on prospects and customers who are more likely to buy specific products and services.

Social Media

Over the past few years, social media scripts have become one of my most effective sales tools. Social media scripts can enable you to extend your lead generation outreach to thousands of targeted prospects rapidly. They can also serve to support the other sales scripts discussed in this chapter. For instance, I often use email invitations to invite my mailing list to social media events.

The email marketing techniques we have previously discussed adapt well to social media, but you must make certain adjustments. One of the biggest adjustments is adapting to a short-text format where visual aids play a significant role. You must also abide by the policies of the social media sites and groups you're using with respect to self-promotion and selling.

Below are a few social media strategies you can use for lead generation, appointment booking, and sales presentations. These strategies can be applied to different social media sites. Some of today's most popular sites include Facebook, LinkedIn, Pinterest, Twitter, and Instagram.

Social Media Lead Generation

Social media can be used to generate leads in a few different ways. One major goal of social media lead generation is to attract followers. Followers are similar to email subscribers in that they subscribe to your social media pages or posts in order to view your content. On some sites, followers can also sign up for groups devoted to specific topics. For instance, I have Facebook groups for sales prospects interested in different topics.

One of the best ways to attract followers is by posting interesting content, similar to the type of content you would post on a blog. It can even be content from your blog. (I'll discuss what kind of content you can post on a blog later in this chapter.) The content can be posted directly in your social media posts if it's short enough to fit the space requirements. For longer content, you can post an attention-getting headline with a link to the full content. Content that includes images tends to get more clicks on sites such as Facebook and Pinterest. Keep in mind that many people will be viewing your content on a smartphone or tablet, and design the look and length accordingly.

Another way to generate leads on social media is to place ads. Social media enables you to target your ads to audiences who meet specific demographic criteria. You can use the ads to drive traffic to your social media site, to your website or blog, or to an offline sales venue.

Both social media posts and ads can be used to promote events such as webinars. One method I use to build my social media following is inviting my followers to events where the event has its own Facebook discussion group. During the event I encourage attendees to interact with each other in the Facebook group, reinforcing their relationship with my prospecting network. The event in turn can invite them to take some action such as visiting a website, signing up for a mailing list, or emailing or phoning me to take advantage of a sales offer.

A fourth way to use social media to generate leads is private messaging. I find that private messaging usually works most effectively if you have built a prior relationship with the person by interacting with them publicly in a discussion group. However, I have also had some success approaching people directly through private messages. When using private messaging to generate leads, keep your messages short enough to be read on a smartphone, with a focus on building trust and rapport in order to elicit some simple action such as exchanging contact information.

Social Media Appointment Setting

Social media scripts can support appointment setting in several ways. One method is inviting your followers to take some appointment-setting action. This can be an invitation to visit an external page to register for a mailing list, an event such as a webinar, or a free consultation. One method I have found works well is inviting webinar audiences to schedule a free consultation with me or one of my sales representatives using a scheduling automation tool called TimeTrade that lets them book an available calendar slot online. Alternately, you can invite social media audiences to email or phone you for an appointment.

You can also use private messages to schedule appointments. For instance, I sometimes invite audiences attending my webinars to private message me on Facebook in order to express interest in learning more about one of my offers. The private conversation can then lead to scheduling a phone call or meeting.

Social Media Presentations

Most social media platforms are not designed to be used to directly deliver sales presentations. However, I have found that they can work well to support sales presentations delivered through other media such as teleconferences and webinars. For instance, when I am delivering teleconferences, I often invite audiences to interact with other listeners on a Facebook group. The Facebook discussion serves to reinforce important elements of my sales presentation, performing functions such as building trust and rapport. Most vitally, it gives me an opportunity to reinforce my call to action by posting information audiences need to respond to my offer, such as website links, email addresses, and phone numbers.

Social Media Follow-up

Social media provides an excellent tool for following up on sales presentations. You can follow up by continuing to post content to your followers and groups. You can also send private messages to follow up with prospects.

Text Media: Blogs, Articles, Books, and Sales Pages

Another powerful set of sales scripting tools is textual media such as blogs, articles, books, and sales pages. What these tools have in common is that they deliver your sales message through the written word. They differ in length, with blogs being the shortest format, articles and sales pages being longer, and books being longest. Articles and books can be delivered through both physical print media such as newspapers and print books and digital media such as online magazines and Kindle. Sales pages can similarly be delivered either digitally or through physical direct mail.

Text Lead Generation

Earlier I mentioned that one way to generate leads on social media is to post content from a blog. You can use a blog, an article, or a book to attract your audience's attention and extend an invitation to provide you with their contact information.

The first step is to pick a topic of interest to your target audience. You can do this by researching your market to identify what topics are most popular with them, what needs they face most frequently, and what problems they most need solved.

You should next select a title of interest to your market. There are a couple approaches to writing titles. The easiest method is to explicitly mention your audience and the problem or solution you plan to cover. An example would be a title like, "Five Ways Senior Citizens Can Lower Their Health Insurance Costs." An alternate approach is to use a title with a more poetic or dramatic ring to it, such as titling a health foods article "Snacks That Give You Heart Attacks." If you are using a digital print medium, you might also consider incorporating popular keywords into your title so that people using search engines can find what you've written.

The structure of your content should parallel the structure of a sales presentation in general, with the specifics adjusted to your specific medium. Your title and opening section serve to generate interest while building trust and rapport. The end of your content should include a call to action serving the purpose of lead generation. For instance, my blog posts often end with an invitation to visit one of my sales pages to learn more information. You might also use a blog post to invite readers to sign up for a mailing list. Similarly, you can use the end of an article or the back of a book to extend an invitation to visit a link or call a phone number.

The length of your content will vary with your medium. Online blogs and articles tend to be upwards of 500 words these days in order to comply with recent Google policy changes targeting low-quality content, but experts disagree on precisely how Google implements its policies. Print article length depends on publisher guidelines for magazines and newspapers. For print books, print-on-demand publishers enable you to publish books as few as 24 pages long, but average length tends to fall somewhere in the range of 100 to 200 pages, and maximum page counts allow even higher . Traditional publishers generally expect nonfiction books to fall in the range of about 200 to 250 pages.

After creating your content, you can use it to generate leads by promoting it to your target audience. Use your social media lists, email list, direct mail list, or phone contact list to let others know about your content.

Text Appointment Setting

Text pieces can include a call to action that facilitates appointment setting. For instance, a blog may end with a link to a page where readers can schedule a free consultation. Similarly, a book can end with a sales page including contact information for scheduling a consultation. You can make this type of offer more compelling by offering readers a special bonus or discount as a thank-you for reading.

Text Presentations

Text media can serve to deliver sales presentations for you. Because readers can read what you write at any time no matter what you're doing, the written word acts as an effective sales multiplier for the number of audience members you're able to reach.

Shorter pieces such as blogs or articles are especially good for addressing key highlights of your sales presentation. For instance, you might write a piece focusing on one specific problem, benefit, or objection. Over a series of blogs or articles, you can deliver multiple elements of your sales presentation to your audience.

A long online sales page or physical direct sales letter gives you room to develop your full sales presentation in written form. The structure should be similar to the AIDA structure discussed above in the section on email sales scripts, but longer. A full-length sales letter may often run as long as 12 printed pages if it intends to cover all the elements in a sales presentation. A full online sales page should be of comparable length. Some sales pages can be shorter if your audience is familiar with you and has been previously exposed to elements in your presentation. Use formatting features such as bolding and boxes to draw attention to key sales highlights. It's especially important to make your call to action prominent. Repeating it in several key locations, including the P.S. of your presentation, is a best practice.

A book gives you the longest space to develop a full sales presentation. Book chapters can elaborate on specific problems, benefits, and objections. In this way a book can also help educate your audience in a way that can support sales presentations delivered through other media.

Text Follow-up

The best way to use textual media for follow-up is to invite readers to continue reading other things you publish. For instance, inviting readers to subscribe to your blog gives you an opportunity to promote to them on an ongoing basis. Similarly, if you use a book to build an email list, you can let audiences know when your next book becomes available.

Multimedia: Audio and Video

Multimedia content is basically similar to text media but adds audio or video components to the presentation. Because of this basic similarity, you can often generate multimedia content by starting with textual content, such as a blog piece, and adding voice narration or visuals. You can also reverse this process by, for instance, starting with an audio recording and then creating a transcript of your recording as the basis for a blog post. This strategy of using one type of content to create content for another medium is called "repurposing" content.

Multimedia Lead Generation

Multimedia content can be used to generate leads in the same way as blog content. In fact, you can often embed multimedia content inside blog posts. For instance, a YouTube video can be embedded in a blog post. You can then promote the video by letting your social media followers or email list know about the blog post.

Another way to create multimedia lead generation content is by broadcasting a podcast. Listeners can subscribe to your podcast similar to the way they subscribe to your email list.

You can also generate leads by distributing physical copies of multimedia content in formats such as CDs and DVDs. This works especially well if you speak at live events such as seminars. You can also offer such physical formats to webinar attendees, email list members, social media followers, or website visitors.

The structure of lead generation multimedia content can be similar to the structure of a lead generation talk or a written blog. The three-chunk formula described earlier lends itself well to this purpose. A simple way to create multimedia lead generation content is to record one of your three-chunk speeches and offer it as an audio or video product.

Multimedia Appointment Setting

Any multimedia lead generation you create can include an invitation to an appointment as part of the presentation. For instance, you can offer a free consultation at the end of the presentation.

Another way to use multimedia for appointment setting is to create a customized video for someone you recently added as a lead. Some marketers I know have had success meeting people at live networking events and following up by sending them customized emails offering to schedule a sales appointment. Some email services let you integrate video into your email.

Multimedia Presentations

There are a few ways you can use multimedia tools to deliver sales presentations. One is to record a sales presentation in audio or video format. An infomercial is an example of this strategy in action. Infomercials usually appear on TV, but you can create your own infomercials using audio or video recording tools.

A more personalized way to use multimedia to give a sales presentation is to deliver a live or recorded virtual presentation using a videoconferencing tool such as Skype or Google Hangouts. Videoconferencing lets you deliver the equivalent of a customized ad to your audience.

Multimedia Follow-up

Multimedia scripts can be used for follow-up in a couple ways. The first way is continuing to create multimedia content and letting your email and social media contacts know about it. A second way is to send customized follow-up video or audio messages.

Exercise

Using the list of types of sales scripts discussed in this chapter, list all the types of sales scripts you are currently using for your lead generation, appointment setting, and sales presentations. Then identify any types of scripts you could start using to increase your leads, book more appointments, or make more sales.

Ideas Into Action

Rick Cooper is a coach, speaker, and trainer who specializes in working with other coaches, speakers, trainers, and consultants. He helps clients increase their visibility online using social media and online marketing, and he also provides done-for-you services such as building websites, lead capture pages, event registration pages, and sales pages.

Rick had first been introduced to sales scripting techniques in college in a class on salesmanship. He later learned some basic sales scripts in his first job out of college selling copiers. However, he didn't realize the power of sales scripts at that time. He didn't take the time to memorize the scripts he had, and he didn't realize he could write his own scripts.

Rick first learned basic sales scripting techniques from me in 2007. He attended a seminar and listed to my teleseminars and audio programs. In 2009 he attended my Sales Scripting Boot Camp in Las Vegas, which he has attended several times since then. This in-depth class proved a real difference-maker in being able to apply my sales scripting techniques and get life-changing results. Rick writes,

> "Since I learned Eric's sales scripting techniques, I truly realized the power of event marketing. I host free teleseminars and webinars where I provide content-rich training and then share an offer at the end of my presentation. Prior to working with Eric, I rarely made a sale from a teleseminar or webinar I hosted. Now, I regularly enroll new clients at the end of my presentations. In fact last year, I led over 80 free teleseminars and webinars. That is how critical the strategy is to my business. I ran a report from October 2011 to April 2015. I had 758 orders totaling $49,511.40. So, that's about $50,000 in revenue I generated from learning Eric's powerful sales scripting techniques. If you want to know how powerful sales scripting is, consider what happened on July 17, 2012. On that date, I delivered a presentation on a conference call to a group of about 60 people that had never heard of me before. I had no trust or rapport with the audience prior to the call. At the end of the call, I offered a program for $47. Over the next hour, 37 people signed up for my program generating $1,739 in sales. They ordered online so I received immediate cash from those sales. And what's great is that many of those clients have gone on to purchase other programs I offer."

Rick adds:

> "Beyond the actual dollars, I would say that sales scripting has given me a higher confidence in my abilities to deliver value and to earn sales. By preparing what I am going to present, I feel more comfortable and relaxed. I build trust and rapport with my audience and I lead them to a next step in working with me. My clients get a lot of value from what I offer, they provide testimonials and come back again and again for my coaching and training. Learning sales scripting techniques from Eric has been a game-changer. I am very grateful to Eric for his help."

Key Points Review

■ Type of sales scripts include face-to-face presentations; front-of-the-room talks; phone calls; email; social media; textual formats such as blogs, articles, and books; and multimedia contexts such as audio and video.

■ Each type of script can be developed for lead generation, appointment booking, or sales presentations.

■ Different types of scripts can interact with each other to support your overall sales funnel.

■ The basic Sales Mountain structure used in face-to-face presentations can be adapted for other media with appropriate modifications.

■ For front-of-the-room talks and comparable media such as teleconferences and webinars, the "$2 Million Formula" three-chunk format works well.

■ For email and textual formats such as sales pages, the AIDA formula is proven effective.

■ Text content such as blog posts can be repurposed for multimedia formats such as audios and videos, and vice versa.

Chapter 12

Borrowing
Successful Scripts

During the 1970s, Japanese car manufacturers quickly displaced over half a century of American dominance by effectively utilizing American methods. The Japanese had learned American manufacturing methods during America's postwar occupation of Japan, when American government representative W. Edwards Deming shared scientific business management techniques with Japanese business leaders. Japanese car manufacturers such as Toyota adapted and refined Deming's methods and combined them with compact car designs borrowed from German auto companies. The result was that when the oil crisis of the 1970s created demand for smaller, more fuel-efficient cars, Japanese companies were in position to overtake traditional American manufacturers of larger vehicles. Later the Korean company Samsung used a similar strategy to overtake Japanese and American competitors in the mobile phone industry. Samsung studied competitors' methods and even contracted to build components for competitors in order to study, learn, and innovate. Samsung's strategy enabled it to rapidly displace established competitors like Motorola and Nokia.

In a similar way, you can rapidly improve your sales scripts by borrowing successful scripts. The fastest way to implement the scripting ideas I've been teaching you in previous chapters is to find existing scripts which already apply these ideas and use them as a baseline to build on. In this chapter I'll give you some tips on how to use this strategy as a shortcut to scripting success.

Have a System to Capture Great Scripting Ideas

The first key is to have a system in place so you are ready to capture great scripting ideas when you encounter them. Great ideas are like sand on the beach: if you don't have a bucket to collect it, it slips through your fingers and is soon left behind and forgotten. To remember your great scripting ideas, create a folder on your computer or mobile device. Be on the lookout for scripting material you can store in your folder. You may encounter scripting ideas when you're watching TV, viewing videos, listening to the radio, scrolling through social media, texting, reading, or driving past a billboard. You may get scripting ideas when you're out shopping at a store or eating at a restaurant. Sometimes your own subconscious will give you script ideas.

Have Your Sales Peers Review Your Scripts

Your sales peers are another great source of scripting ideas. Other people at your company or in your industry may have more sales experience than you or different sales experience than you. They may already be using successful scripting techniques. Ask them to review your scripts and suggest ideas and improvements. If they're willing, invite them to role play your scripts with you or listen in on your interaction with prospects in order to give you feedback.

Borrow Other People's Scripts

Professional ad writers, called "copywriters," use what they call "*swipe files*." A swipe file is a file of successful ads that serve as templates which can be customized to create new ads. Copywriters build their swipe files by collecting ads from newspapers, magazines, junk mail, radio, TV, and the Internet. They look for examples of compelling headlines, powerful sales vocabulary, persuasive closes, and other sales script elements. They also collect files of graphic design elements such as images and logos that accompany successful scripts. Additionally, they study supporting sales elements such as direct-mail response mechanisms and website templates.

One way to build your swipe file is to ***borrow other people's scripts in your industry***. Look at the scripts your top competitors are already using. Use these for a baseline. Then customize them for your product or service and improve them by applying persuasion engineering techniques.

Another way to build your swipe file is to ***borrow other people's scripts in other industries***. My marketing mentor Jay Abraham stresses the value of studying what people in other industries are doing as a way to inspire fresh ideas you can apply to your own industry. Often your competitors are only paying attention to your own industry and overlooking techniques other industries are using successfully, giving you an opportunity to gain an advantage. For instance, Apple pioneered the digital music download industry by releasing the iPod in 2001 and opening the iTunes Store in 2003, giving it an early lead that has enabled it to survive competition from streaming services like Pandora and Spotify. I saw that other industries were delivering virtual training successfully, so I adapted this to the sales industry, gaining an edge over competitors who have yet to adopt this technology. In the same way you can borrow scripts from other industries.

Collect Convincers

Another type of scripting material you should collect is ***convincers***. A convincer is a third-party endorsement of a point you're trying to make in your sales presentation. A third-party endorsement carries more objective weight than a claim you make on your own authority alone. Convincers come in a variety of forms.

Testimonials are convincers consisting of quotes from your satisfied customers. There are a couple major categories of testimonials. Some testimonials testify to your brand as a whole, telling others about your quality, reliability, superior service, or great value. Other testimonials testify to a specific product or service you offer.

Quotes can also come from other experts or celebrities. For instance, you might find a quote from a well-known expert who makes a statement supporting a point you're trying to make in your sales presentation. I sometimes quote basketball star Michael Jordan to inspire my sales students with Jordan's championship mindset.

Case studies can provide dramatic stories about the results people got when they used your product or service or experienced a related situation. For example, I collect case studies about my sales students and the successes they have experienced using my system. You can cite case studies to illustrate a problem, benefit, objection response, or another point you want to make.

Statistics give you hard numbers to back up your points. For instance, McDonald's signs display how many hamburgers the fast-food chain has served since it opened in the 1940s. In 2013 McDonald's was on track to serve its 300 billionth hamburger. The cover of the first edition of my book *The System* mentioned I had trained over 10,000 students, a number which continues to rise. This type of specific number carries more weight than if I had just said I'd trained a lot of students.

Articles can provide you with quotes, case studies, statistics, and other persuasive information. An advantage of citing articles is that you borrow the authority of the publisher. When you can quote a source such as *The New York Times* or *TIME Magazine*, this lends name recognition to your statement.

Books can lend similar authority to your presentation. Book authors are perceived as experts. When you cite a book to support your claim, you invoke expert credibility. You can cite books by recognized experts, or you can write your own book to position yourself as an expert.

Audios can enhance your presentation by adding the sound of your voice or another person's voice to the words of your script. A recorded voice carries a tone of authority similar to that of a radio announcer. You can record yourself, or you can play recordings of known figures to enhance your presentations. Many TV commercials use a variation of this technique by playing popular songs in the background. Microsoft licensed the Rolling Stones classic "Start Me Up" to showcase Windows' then-new "start" button feature when the company launched Windows 95 in 1995. The A-ha song "Take on Me" has appeared in commercials from GEICO and Volkswagen over the past few years. Chrysler used a song from Detroit-area musician Eminem for its 2011 Super Bowl ad.

Videos can bring your sales presentation to life visually. Videos can dramatize stories about someone who had a problem that was solved by your product or service. Commercials that tell before-and-after stories illustrate this technique. Another way to use videos effectively is for product demonstrations, a technique often seen in ads for exercise products.

Exercise

Create a folder called "Borrowed Scripts" where you can start collecting borrowed sales scripts. Include any subfolders you want, such as "Convincers." Get in the habit of using this folder to save scripts you encounter in your junk mail, in your email, on the Internet, or from other sources. You can include ads you scan in from newspapers and magazines. Give each script you save a descriptive name so you can easily find it again.

Ideas Into Action

David Turner is a musician. People hire him to play the piano at their functions. Prior to meeting me, David struggled financially like a lot of musicians and artists do. David applied my sales scripting ideas to help him book more gigs. It also gave him the confidence to raise his fees. As a result, David has made more money in the last five years than he had in the previous 20 combined. David is also debt-free now!

Key Points Review

- The fastest way to create successful scripts is to copy successful scripts.

- Have a system to capture great scripting ideas.

- Have your sales peers review your scripts.

- Borrow other people's scripts by building "***swipe files***" from other people in your industry and other industries.

- Collect convincers such as testimonials, quotes, and case studies.

Chapter 13

Sample Scripts

In the last chapter, I talked about how borrowing successful scripts can help you generate your own scripts faster. Now I'm going to give you a few sample scripts to help you put this distinction into action. In this chapter I'll give you some examples of scripts for a variety of situations:

- Face-to-face presentations
- Front-of-the-room talks
- Phone calls
- Email
- Blogs
- Videos

The appendices will include additional sample script resources.

Face-to-Face Sales Scripts

Scripts for face-to-face sales presentation form the backbone of an effective sales system. Here are some examples of scripts I and my trainers use during sales presentations that you can adapt to your own selling situation.

Scripts for Building Trust and Rapport

Stories are one of the best ways to build trust and rapport. Here's an example of a story script that has proven effective in my sales experience. I call this story "The Arvee Robinson Story."

> When Arvee Robinson met Eric Lofholm she had a resistance to selling. Arvee is a small business owner. When she met Eric she was earning about $4,000 per month. She has a website. She markets to clients over the phone, giving speeches, and giving conference calls. Eric shared the idea of growing her business using sales scripts. Initially she had a huge resistance to scripting. Although she was skeptical she was interested in increasing her results. Eric first helped Arvee work on her script for getting coaching clients. The presentation she was using did not build enough value in the coaching service she offered. Eric taught her how to create a great presentation. Arvee now has a full practice and she doubled her fees. Her income has increased in some months to over $15,000 per month as a direct result of what she has learned from Eric. Arvee recently purchased a home because of her increase in sales. What is great for Arvee is she has the script for the rest of her life. The script will make Arvee over $500,000 in coaching fees.

Scripts for Probing Questions

Here are a few scripts you can use for the probing questions section of your presentation:

> For me to best help you Mr. Prospect I need to ask you a few questions. Would that be OK?
>
> For me to best help you I have created a list of questions to go over with you. Would it be OK if I went over these questions and took notes?
>
> What is your true need in regards to _____?

Scripts for Benefits

Back in Chapter 5 I mentioned that there are five different types of benefits which can enter into your sales scripts:

- Tangible benefits
- Intangible benefits
- The benefit of taking action

- The consequences of not taking action
- Benefit of the benefit

Here are some scripts you can use to communicate each of these types of benefits.

Tangible Benefits

Tangible benefits are benefits that produce definable results. Here are some common examples:

> Make you more money
> Decrease employee turnover
> Live longer
> Save you money
> Save you time

Intangible Benefits

Intangible benefits are benefits that you can't measure. For example:

> Increased confidence
> Peace of mind
> Have more energy

Benefits of Taking Action

This is focusing the prospect on how they are going to benefit by purchasing your produce or service. Here's an example you may have seen on TV:

> If you order now, you'll get this special bonus, valued at $39.99, absolutely free with your order. This offer is only good for the next 15 minutes, so call or visit our website now.

Consequences of Not Taking Action

This is focusing your prospect on the consequences of not taking action. This technique is used to sell life insurance. The salesperson focuses your attention

on the consequences to you and your family if you don't have life insurance.
Here's an example from insurance sales master Ben Feldman, as recounted in
Andrew Thomson's book *The Feldman Method*:

> Do you want your little boy to go to school? It isn't the policy that costs money, it's the education that costs money. May I talk to you about doing something about it? Which is cheaper, paying for your child's education in four years—or in 18 years? You have 18 years to pay for his education—if you begin *now*. You *can't* begin now? Then you'll have to pay for it all at once! Tell me—could you—right now—pay for his first year of college?

Benefit of the Benefit

The benefit of the benefit is how the prospect benefits from the main benefit of
your product or service. Let's say your product helps your customers save
$10,000 per month in expenses. The $10,000 savings is the main benefit. Here's
a short script you might use to drive home the benefit from saving $10,000:

> In what ways will saving $10,000 help you?
>
> [Listen for the prospect's answer. For instance, they might say their wife could quit her job. Then follow up:]
>
> What would that mean?

Scripts for Closing

Your closing script is often what makes or breaks your sale. Over the years I
have adapted, developed, and tested a wide variety of closing scripts. Here are
some of my favorites.

Down Payment Close

> I understand that you don't have the $6,000 to get started today. Why don't you put down $1,000? We will get you started and work out payments on the rest.

Spouse Close

This close applies if they say they need to speak to their spouse before making
a decision.

> Sign up today. If after speaking with your spouse, if they don't want you to do it simply call me and we can cancel your order.

Recommendation Close

This close works well after a free consultation where you have gathered information about your prospect's needs.

> Here is my recommendation. [Share recommendation.] Would you like to move forward?

Reduce the Risk Close

> Instead of ordering $10,000 today why don't you just order $500? You can try us out. After you have used up you inventory you can then place a larger order. Sound good?

Guarantee Close

> Our product guarantees results. If after 30 days you are not fully satisfied for any reason I will refund you investment. What do you say we give it a try?

Quote Close (Proposal close)

> Send your prospect over a proposal. Follow up with them and ask them if they would like to move forward.

Reduce It to the Ridiculous Close

> The program is only $300 for the year. That is less than $30 per month. That is less than $1.00 per day. As I mentioned the program is fully guaranteed. You have nothing to lose and everything to gain. What do you say we give it a try?

Assume the Sale

> We are going out for crab tonight so I need you to be ready at 7:00.
> Where would you like your desk delivered?
> What day would you like me to start?
> Which credit card will you be using today?
> Sign here please.
> How many months are you going to start off with?

Fill out the Paperwork Close

What is you mailing address? What is your email address? What is your phone number? What is your credit card number?

Alternate of Choice Close

I am available on Tuesday at 2:00 or Wednesday at 2:00. What would work best for you?

Ask

Would you like to schedule an appointment today?

How Do You Feel Close

How do you feel about scheduling an appointment today?
How do you feel about helping me out with a few referrals today?
How do you feel about getting started today?

Would You Feel Comfortable Close

This is a very soft way of closing. Simply deliver this close and then remain silent:

Would you feel comfortable moving forward today?

Ask a Question for Commitment and Be Silent Close

Would you like to buy some Girl Scout Cookies?

Take Away

This is where you offer the prospect a deal and then you take the deal away. You demand action or the deal is off.

The special is good until 5:00 today. I need an answer now or the price I quoted you will no longer be good. I am looking at two houses. I need an answer now or I am going to go with the other house.

Sample Close for Selling a Program

Here is an example of how to build some of these closing techniques into a closing script for selling a program.

> At the _____ (name of the program) _____ (instructor name) will teach you how to get publicity in the newspaper, on the radio, on TV and the internet. The program is on _____ in _____ (say city seminar is in). At the program you will learn: Share 5 benefits. Follow each benefit with the script – what that means to you is... The investment is $_____. As a bonus for signing up you will receive 1._____ 2._____ 3._____ The program is backed by a 100% money back guarantee. If after attending the program you are unhappy for any reason we will refund your tuition 100%. Lastly we have a $_____ early bird discount making your total investment only $_____. Would you like to register for the program?

Scripts for Objection Handling

Objection handling scripts can boost your closing rate by helping you recover sales you would have otherwise lost. Because objection handling scripts are so valuable, I've developed over a dozen different categories and written many scripts in each category. Here are some examples you can borrow.

Story

One of the most powerful was to handle an objection is with a story. One way to start off the story is by saying,

> That reminds me of a story of a client who was in a similar situation. Let me share with you what they did. . .

Here's an example of how to build a story into a script. Imagine you just delivered a close for a health product that costs $100 per month. The Prospect says the price is too high. You ask them if, other than the price, is there anything else preventing them from moving forward (using the technique of isolating the objection). After you let them respond, you introduce the story to handle the objection:

> Let me share with you a story I recently heard from a friend of mine named Eric. Eric's car battery needed to be replaced. He told his wife he would be dropping his car off at

their local mechanics to have it done. He was going to get a ride from the mechanics to his office from one of his co-workers so she didn't need to worry about giving him a ride. She expected the battery would cost between $50 and $75.

About an hour after Eric dropped off the car his mechanic called him to let him know the regular services needed to be done on his car. The mechanic mentioned to Eric that since the car was already here he might as well get the servicing done. Eric agreed. About 2 hours later the mechanic called back to let Eric know while he was doing the servicing he noticed the brakes needed repair. Again, he suggested to Eric since the car is already here he might as well have the brakes done. Again, Eric agreed.

Around 4 o'clock Eric picked up the car. The total bill was around $350. On the way home Eric called his wife to let her know about the $350 charge on their debit card. Eric's wife handles the bank account so he wanted to let her know about the charge. When his wife heard the bill was $350 she was puzzled. She said to Eric I thought a battery was between $50-$75. Eric then told her about the maintenance. She said $350, now that is expensive. Eric responded by saying actually it is extremely inexpensive. He told his wife the most inexpensive way to maintain a car is to do regular maintenance. The most expensive way to maintain a car is to fix it when it breaks down. Now that can cost thousands of dollars.

Your health is no different. The most inexpensive way to maintain your health is to do preventative maintenance. The most expensive way is to wait until something is wrong like needing to have your gallbladder taken out. If 18 you really think about it your health is priceless would you agree? [Let them respond.]

My product is only $100 per month. You can expect to be healthier, have more energy and it is a preventative maintenance to help eliminate problems before they even come up. What do you say we give it a try? [Let them respond.]

Question

You can answer an objection with a question. For example:

Objection: *The price is too high.*

Response: By too high what exactly do you mean?

Response: How much too much is it?

Response: Compared to what?

Objection: *I don't have the time.*

Response: When will you have the time?

Response: On a scale of 1-10 how motivated are you to move forward?

Response: What do you mean by that?

Solve the Problem

One way to handle an objection is to solve the problem.

If you were in the network marketing business you might invite a prospect to a hotel meeting on a Wednesday night. The prospect might say they can't get a babysitter. You could solve the problem by offering to have your sister babysit.

Isolate

Isolating the objection is one of my favorite techniques. I like it because it is very effective and easy to learn. Here are some examples of scripts using this technique:

> **Objection:** I don't have the money.
>
> **Response:** I can appreciate that. Other than the money is there anything else that is preventing you from taking action today? [After they respond, ask a closing question and be silent.]
>
> **Objection:** I don't have the time.
>
> **Response:** Other than the time, is there anything else preventing you from moving forward today?

Bring out the Objection

This is another very simple, yet very powerful technique. Bring out the objection is the opposite of isolate. Often times the true objection is a nonstated objection. Many times the prospect will not reveal the true objection. In this case, each objection that they give you is actually a stall, not an objection. When you use this technique it encourages the prospect to be honest with you. Here are some examples:

> **Objection:** I don't have the money.
>
> **Response:** I understand. So what you are saying is that you don't have the money. Is that correct? [Let them respond.]
>
> I am sure that you have some other concerns before moving forward. Do you mind sharing those other concerns with me? Let them respond.
>
> **Objection:** I need to think about it.
>
> **Response:** I understand. Other than thinking about it I am sure that you have some other concerns. Do you mind sharing those other concerns with me?

Script the Most Common Objections

You can develop scripted responses to each objection. Here is an example:

> **Objection:** *I need to speak to my wife.*
>
> **Response:** I understand. So if your wife says yes, does that mean that you will do it? [Let them respond yes.] Let me ask you a different question, what if she says no? [At this point introduce a trial close by asking a question for commitment and then remaining silent.]

Investigate

Here is a script you can use after many objections:

> Tell me more about that.

Before It Comes up

This is one of the most powerful objection handling techniques. You can reverse engineer your sales presentation to anticipate the objections that the prospect might bring up. You then can address the objections in the body of the sales presentation.

Here is an example of this technique in action. One of my clients sells $6,000 wealth building seminars. One of the objections they encounter is, "I am already a millionaire. What do I need your program for?"

One of the scripts I created to handle this objection goes like this:

> I am sure you are familiar with Donald Trump. Is that true? [Let them respond.]
>
> Would you agree that he is a great businessman? [Let them respond.]
>
> After Trump became a multi millionaire he made some bad financial decisions. In fact he lost so much money he went upside down $900 million. One day Trump was walking in downtown Manhattan with his then wife Marla Maples. He said, "Marla, you see that bum right there. He is worth $900 million more than I am."
>
> Although Trump is a great businessman, he made some huge mistakes when it came to wealth building. If Trump was a client of ours we could have helped prevent him from losing his wealth.
>
> It is great that you have a net worth in the millions. We help clients like you not only increase your wealth but also preserve it. Some of our top clients are multimillionaires like yourself.

Share the Benefits

Objections are an opportunity to share the benefits. If the prospect says that insurance is not a good investment you can show them how it is a great investment.

Reduce the Risk

This means to change the offer. For instance, if you were asking for a 6 month commitment, reduce the risk for the prospect by reducing the term to 3 months.

Be Unreasonable

This means to make an unreasonable request. For example ask the prospect to get a second job so they can purchase your product or service. Suggest that they sell their car.

Negotiate

You can change the deal by negotiating. If I do this, will you do that? For example:

> If I lower the price by 5%, will you move forward today?

What Would Need to Happen?

Close the sale by asking a question.

> What would need to happen in order for you to move forward today?
> What would need to happen in order to get a check today?

Price Objection Handling Scripts

If they say, "The price is too high," here are a number of ways you can respond:

> How much too much is it?
> Other than the price is there anything else preventing you from moving forward?
> Tell me more about that?
> Other than the price I am sure that you have some other concerns. Do you mind sharing your other concerns?

That reminds me of story of a client that had the same concern you do. They thought the price was too high also. I let them know that although $695 can be considered a lot of money on one hand it will cost them more money by not doing the program. They thought about it and said the program is backed by a money back guarantee so alright let's give it a try. Last month this client made over $11,000 on a single idea they got from the program. Isn't that great? [Let them respond.] I know the program will really help you. What do you say we give it a try?

Is that your only concern?

Public Speaking Sales Scripts

Back in Chapters 7 and 11 I shared my template for a front-of-the-room talk where you have 30 minutes to an hour to deliver your presentation. But sometimes you will only have a few minutes to speak. In this case, you can deliver a very brief presentation with a call to action. Here is an example:

Good afternoon everyone. [Let them respond.]

My name is Eric Lofholm. I am only here for a few minutes today. My topic is time management. How many of you would like to learn some great ideas on time management?

Here are two quick ideas.

Plan your day on paper before the day starts. Every time management guru agrees it is a good idea to plan your day on paper before the day starts. How many of you have found that when you write down what you want to accomplish you take more action by a show of hands?

The second idea is this. What I have found is time management is about asking and answering questions in writing. Once I realized this I decided to make a list of questions to plan an optimum day. So when I plan I just ask and answer these 10 questions. [Hold up piece of paper with the questions on it.]

By doing this I get more done, take more action and create better results. How many of you would like a copy of my questions so you could create your own list of questions by a show of hands? Great.

Under your chair is an index card. Take a moment right now and write your name and email address legibly. I will have the questions emailed out to you tomorrow.

Go ahead and pass the cards to the center.

Thank you for your time.

Phone Sales Scripts

Here's an example of a phone script you can use for appointment setting:

Who would I speak with in regards to being a guest speaker at your office?

You would need to speak with _____?

Can you transfer me please?

Hi this is _____?

Hi _____, how are you today? Let them respond.

This is Eric Lofholm. I am the president of Eric Lofholm International. We are a San Diego based sales training firm. The reason for the call today is I am teaching a 1 day sales mastery seminar in your area. Because of that event I am coming to offices like yours and doing 30-45 minute complimentary sales trainings on the topic of your choice. Popular topics are Time Management, How to Close, and how to Set Unlimited Appointments. How do you feel about me being a guest speaker at one of your upcoming sales meetings?

Here's a script for running an appointment over the phone:

Hi is _____ [say prospect's name] in?

Hi _____ [say prospect's name] this is _____ [say your name] calling for your sales consultation. How are you today?

Great. Here is how our call is going to go today. I am going to give you a brief overview of Eric Lofholm International. Then I will ask you some questions to get to know you and your business better. Then at the end of the call I will share with you how we can help you make more money with your selling. Sound good? [Let them respond.]

Do you have any questions before we get started? [Let them respond.]

Let me share with you a little bit about Eric Lofholm International. What we are about is helping our clients achieve their business dream or big business goal. We believe that in order to achieve a business dream or big business goal that you need a sales system. Our founder, Eric Lofholm, started our company on a dream to become a top speaker like Zig Ziglar. This business dream has given Eric the motivation to grow the business to where we now have clients all over the world that we are helping achieve their business dreams. The foundation of our success is our sales systems

Our company was founded in 1999.

Our mission is to help our clients make progress towards their business dream by applying sales systems.

Now I would like to ask you some questions so I can get to know you better. Do you have a dream you want to accomplish in your business?

Can you share what your dream is?

What do you sell?

How long have you been selling?

How is it going?

How did you learn about Eric?

Have you ever attended any of our live seminars?

Have you ever received professional sales training before?

What I would like to do now is a quick sale skills assessment with you.

How would you rate yourself in closing on a scale of 1-10?

How would you rate yourself in objection handling on a scale of 1-10? How would you rate yourself in appointment setting on a scale of 1-10? How would you rate yourself in referrals on a scale of 1-10?

How would you rate yourself in follow up on a scale of 1-10?

How would you rate yourself in recruiting (if MLM) on a scale of 1-10? How would you rate yourself in taking action on a scale of 1-10?

Do you currently use sales systems to grow your business?

What is your biggest sales challenge?

What would it mean to you if you solved this challenge?

What will it cost you if you don't?

[Tell your story.]

[Share some content here. Give ideas on how they can increase their results. Share other success stories here.]

What I would like to do now is share with you my recommendation of how we can best help you. The program I am going to recommend is Silver Protégé.

In the Silver Protégé Program you will receive all of the tools and resources you need to take your career to the next level.

Do you have internet access?

Go to www.silverprotege.com and scroll down to where it says

The program is called the Unstoppable Selling System.

The Silver Protégé Program includes:

1. Weekly live sales training call for 1 year
2. Private Facebook Group
3. Certification
4. 12 Audio Modules
5. Life by Design 2 day boot camp or 4 week Life by Design Webinar
6. Membership website that is mobile friendly

The special we are running right now is I can upgrade you to a lifetime membership. The program is normally a 1-year program. What that means is you can stay in the program as long as you want without any additional fees or dues.

Next you can add up to 3 family members at no additional investment. All we ask is they are on your family tree. Brother, sister, cousin, mom, uncle, etc.—in-laws are fine as well as the step side of your family.

The program is $1,295.

The regular special is $500

The extra special we are running now is $299. Would you like to take advantage of the special?

The payment plan is $150 down and $50 per month for 4 months.

Here's another example of a phone script you can use to follow up with someone you gave a presentation to who didn't buy:

Hi is _____ in? [Let them respond.]

Hi _____, this is _____ [your name] calling from _____ [your company]. How are you today? [Let them respond.]

The reason for the call is you recently attended my talk about _____(topic of talk) and I wanted to follow up with you.

[Ask questions like:]

How did you find out about the presentation?

What did you like most about it?

What idea did you find the most useful?

At the end of the speech I made a terrific offer. Were you interested in the offer?

What did you like most about it?

What was the reason you didn't move forward?

Would you like to move forward now?

When you call here are some different possible outcomes you can prepare scripts for:

- The customer buys from you just because you followed up and asked.
- The customer agrees to buy from you at a later date when the money comes in.
- The customer agrees to a payment plan.
- The customer purchases a smaller product.
- The customer does not buy but wants a follow up call at a later date.
- The customer does not buy.

Email Sales Scripts

Here's an example of an email script I've used that has generated sales consistently in various forms:

Subject line:

I am looking for 7 people to sprint with me in July, Aug, and Sept!

Body:

Dear [First Name],

I am looking for 7 people to sprint with me in July, August, and September!

I am at a very exciting time in my business and in my life right now. I am highly, highly motivated to sprint like I have never sprinted before and I am looking for 7 people who would like to sprint along side of me!

Do you want to have a GREAT 3rd quarter…possibly the best quarter of your career? If yes, this program could be perfect for you!

I am looking for people who want to accomplish extraordinary during the 3rd quarter!!

If you know me then you know I am famous for making irresistible offers. This is truly an irresistible offer!! I am going to blow you away with what I have put together!!

The timing couldn't be more perfect. July 1 is right around the corner. July 1 is the first day of the second half of the year.

I am looking to produce the best results I have ever produced during the 3rd quarter of this year and I want to help you do the same.

I will be doing a conference call on Friday, June 20 at 9 am to go over all the details. The phone number to use is [phone]. The pin code is [code].

If you are unable to make the live call you can request a copy of the recording by sending an email to eric@ericlofholm.com and put "Sales Champion 7" in the subject line. Include your name and number in the body of the email and I will send you a copy of the recording.

Success,

Eric Lofholm

Social Media Sales Scripts

My Internet marketing consultant Rick Cooper specializes in generating leads, booking appointments, and making sales using social media scripts. Here are a few scripts Rick has taught my sales students during guest presentations for my Gold Protégé calls:

New blog post on _____. Tips to _____. Read it now at: _____.

I created a Free Report on _____. This information is for people who want to _____. To request a copy, send me a Private Message on Facebook.

Interested in learning how to _____? Here's a Video I recorded on how to _____. Watch it Now!

Join me for a Free Conf Call/Webinar on _____. Learn how to _____. Register online at: _____.

I'm going to an event on _____ hosted by _____. I'm excited to see the speaker _____ who will talk about _____. I have an extra ticket to the event. Let me know if you're interested in attending.

Hi _____. Thanks for connecting. I meet a lot of people through networking. Who makes a good referral for you?

Hi _____. I'm reaching out to business owners in the area who are interested in working together to support each other. Are you interested in talking about ways to help each other out?

Sample Blog Scripts

Here's an example of a blog script I used for lead generation:

> In my last blog post I shared some golden nuggets on goal setting to help you achieve your goals this year. To put this into practice, one of the keys to translating goals into action is effective time management, so in my next few blogs I'm going to be sharing some of my top time management tips. In this blog I'm going to teach you some tips for thinking like a time management master.
>
> ### How My Time Management Mindset Changed
>
> While I consider myself a time management expert now, that wasn't always the case. In my early twenties, I was a cook at McDonald's earning $5.00 an hour. That's what an hour was worth to me. But then I invested some time in learning and mastering top-level sales training skills and growing my own sales training business. Today my time is over a hundred times more valuable than it was when I worked at McDonald's.
>
> What changed? Time didn't change: there's still the same number of hours in the day. The big change was my mindset about my ability to manage time. I realized that I can choose what I do with my time, and by choosing to focus my time on more valuable activities, I can earn more from the same number of work hours.
>
> Here's another way to explain it: time management is about time choices. The better time choices you make, the more successful you'll become. My success has grown steadily since I made a decision years ago to focus more time on my top revenue-producing activities: generating leads, booking appointments, and running sales presentations. Over the last few years I've identified new ways to leverage my time through outsourcing, automation and other time-efficient strategies. The value I generate per hour keeps increasing because of how I choose to invest my time.
>
> ### Cultivating the Mindset of a Time Management Master
>
> The change I'm describing above illustrates a shift in mindset. As with every aspect of sales and business, you must develop the proper mindset to make a new strategy work for you. Many people believe that they're not good at time management. They believe that they're great at procrastinating. If you want to shift away from the mindset of a procrastinator to the mindset of a time management master, say the following affirmations each day to improve your inner game:
>
> *Each day, I'm getting better and better at time management.*
>
> *I am a master of action.*
>
> *I am a time management master.*
>
> *I consistently plan my day before the day starts.*

(You can say each affirmation every day, or say one over and over and then switch after you've conditioned that one.)

Time Management Affirmation in Action

Years ago, during a time management discussion in a seminar, one of my students, Joey Azsterbaum, raised his hand and told me flat-out that he had terrible time management skills. I said, "Joey, if you say it like that, I believe you. So, do you want to improve your time management?"

He said yes, so I suggested that he use the following affirmations over and over each day:

> *I am a time management master.*
>
> *He is a time management master.*
>
> *Joey is a time management master.*

Why did I have Joey say this three different ways? Persuasion psychology expert Dr. Donald Moine taught me that if you affirm a statement in the first person and third person as well as with your name, it impacts the subconscious mind in different ways.

A few months later, when another one of my clients met Joey, he was amazed at his efficiency and action, so he asked Joey how he was able to be so productive. Joey said, "Well, it's quite simple: I'm a time management master." He had literally reprogrammed his subconscious to believe that he is a master of time management. If you ever meet Joey, you can ask him about that, and he will tell you that he is a master of time management.

Time Management Truths

Once you have the proper time management mindset, you can apply what I consider key time management truths:

> *We all have the same amount of time.*
>
> *Time can have a future value, like interest from money you invest at a bank.*
>
> *Some activities produce better results than others.*

Let's look at some applications of these truths. As I began to learn more and more about time, I discovered the importance of understanding the value of an hour. To calculate the worth to you of an hour financially, take how much money you earn annually and divide this by the number of hours that you work per year. Generally speaking, if you work full-time, you work 2,000 hours per year (fifty weeks a year times forty hours a week). If you earn $100,000 a year and you work 2,000 hours per year, an hour is worth $50 to you. (You may work more or less than forty hours, so adjust your numbers according to your situation.)

If you play with these numbers, one thing you'll notice is that, because your annual revenue is directly proportionate to the value you earn per hour, you can dramatically increase your annual revenue by increasing your productivity. For instance, if you earn $50,000 annually and work 2,000 hours a year, an extra hour of productivity per work day is worth $6,250 to you per year, or $62,500 over ten years. If you earn $100,000 a year, the value of an extra hour a day doubles to $12,500 a year or $125,000 in ten years.

Understanding an hour's financial worth to you provides a great starting point for you to begin to make better time management choices. The person who cleans my home charges me $75 for each visit. It probably takes her and her crew three hours to complete the job. If I was to do the work myself, and it took me three hours, then I'd be earning $25 an hour. An hour to me is much more valuable than $25. Hence, that's why I hire her and her team to do it.

Here's a key time management principle that focuses directly on this idea of understanding the value of an hour:

Do what you do best and pay others to do the rest.

Pretty simple, huh? Yet you'll be amazed at how understanding the value of an hour will help you prioritize tasks and activities

To Learn More

The tips in this blog are taken from a complete program I teach on time management. You can learn more about my time management tips by continuing to follow this blog, or by checking out my Unstoppable Selling System program, where I teach my full time management step-by-step system.

Sample Video Scripts

Here's a script I've used for my website sales page to support the text and order form on the page:

Hi, my name is Eric Lofholm, and thanks for stopping by. I've been helping people just like you make more sales for more than ten years. And for years I taught seminars. And after teaching a great seminar, I'd also be left with a little sense of frustration. Frustration knowing that although you get pumped up and excited and filled with great content, I knew that my clients needed more. And this is why I created the Silver Protégé program. I believe that this is the finest work-from-home sales mentor program that exists in the world at any price. In the Silver Protégé program, you have the opportunity to be mentored by me on a weekly basis. And the way that I train you is 30 minutes a week. All it takes to turn you into a sales champion is 30 minutes a week.

Napoleon Hill in the book *Think and Grow Rich* talks about the importance of people that are in sales or need sales skills to be motivated on a weekly basis. So every Thursday we come together on a conference call for a half an hour, and I will pour into you great content, sales training ideas, motivational strategies, and self-esteem to help uplift you to a higher level of success.

If you're unable to make the live call, every call is recorded, and you'll have access to listen to that call through your computer, or you can burn it on an audio CD and you can listen to it in your car, or you can watch it through our membership website.

What's included in the Silver Protégé program is a weekly live call; all the notes with all the key ideas are emailed out to you or you'll have access to them on our membership website. Every call is recorded. You'll also have access to my four-week Sales Mountain webinar where I teach you step-by-step how to create a great presentation that closes. This is the most content-rich webinar that I teach. You'll also receive my eight-audio program called the Eric Lofholm Persuasion and Influence System. This is my most content-rich audio program. It contains over seven hours of my best ideas. Lastly, you'll get instant access to my membership website. This allows you to train 24 hours a day, 7 days a week, whenever it's convenient for you. The membership website is loaded with over 100 hours of sales training content.

By filling out the form below and signing up for the program right now, you will get instant access to our membership website with over 100 hours of great training content.

You'll also be eligible to participate in my next training call, which is every Thursday. You can plug in this coming Thursday and start training with me by having me be your sales coach.

I encourage you to take action right now. Fill out the form below. Register for the program and allow me to mentor you in your sales over the next twelve months.

The scripts in this chapter are just a few samples. Use the techniques from Chapter 12 to collect more and begin building your own script library.

Exercise

Pick one of the sample scripts included in this chapter. Use it as a template to create a script with the same structure for one of your own products or services.

Ideas Into Action

For the last decade Judy O'Higgins has been an independent distributor for an online greeting card and gift company designed for business owners and professionals to increase their customer retention and referrals. Before she started taking courses with me in 2008 she had never received any professional sales training. She began using my scripting techniques to acquire new customers and to build a team of distributors. Since adopting my scripting techniques, she has grown her team to well over 5,000 and has achieved the current rank of #16 in her company out of 166,000 total distributors.

Judy writes, "I first became involved with Eric around 2008 when I was taught the stages, or steps, to a successful sale. That was life-changing in itself, and I learn and teach those vital steps today. Next, I took Eric's course on scripting and developed distinct words for what to say when speaking to a prospective customer and also a prospective new team member. The scripts have been refined and modified over the years, but their vital importance has not changed. Now I know and can teach what to say during each step of the prospecting process—the very thing that stops many network marketers and causes them to quit— because they didn't know what to say. . . Scripting works, and should be widely accepted as a critical sales skill both in the network marketing profession and in the bigger arena of all business models."

Key Points Review

Adapt the scripts in this chapter and others you collect to help speed up the process of writing your own scripts.

Chapter 14

Scripting GSA (Goals, Strategy, Action)

This chapter contains one of the five best business-building ideas I know. It's a strategy that can be applied to any area of business. Here I'm going to apply it to scripting.

I first learned the GSA distinction from my first business mentor, Dante Perano, a real estate investor. About twenty years ago as I was just getting started on my career, I attended a seminar where Dante was sharing real estate investment strategies. During his talk, he shared a story about an idea from J. Paul Getty's book, *How to Be Rich*.

Getty was once the wealthiest man in the world. Late in his career, he wrote his book sharing his success secrets. According to Dante, Getty not only revealed his formula for wealth, he stated that if you applied this formula, you too could have anything you want in life.

Since I was then working a day job at McDonald's while attending community college, my initial reaction was skeptical. I thought to myself, *Come on, how could one idea allow you to create whatever you wanted in your life?* But I was also curious, and I still wanted to hear what Getty's formula was.

The formula contained three letters: GSA, which stands for Goal, Strategies, and Action. Dante told us all that day, "All you need to do is ask yourself what do I want, then develop the strategy to achieve this, then take massive action on a daily basis."

I thought about this. Even though I was still skeptical, a few months later I decided to try the idea out. I asked myself, "What do I want?"

The first thing that popped into my head was this: "Quit working at McDonald's."

So I quit. The second thing that popped into my head was that I no longer wanted to attend college. I had been attending for five years and had yet to complete two years' worth of credits. College wasn't for me. I made a decision right then to quit school.

The third thing that popped into my head was this: I wanted to communicate to the woman I was dating how much I cared for her. So what did I do? I went over and proposed to her on one knee at our favorite park in Rocklin, California, wearing my McDonald's uniform. (My wife told me years later, "I always knew I'd marry a man in uniform. I just didn't know it would be a McDonald's uniform.")

I made those three decisions in one single day. My life, and ultimately my destiny, changed after having made those three decisions.

I've continued to apply the GSA distinction ever since Dante first told that story over twenty years ago. I've taught this concept to tens of thousands of people, and I've found it to be one of the five best business building ideas I've ever learned. In the remainder of this chapter, I am going to focus on how you can apply this idea to scripting, the most powerful sales strategy I've ever learned. Perhaps combing these ideas will have a similar impact on you as it's had on me through all these years.

GSA: Goals Strategy Action

The first part of GSA is Goals. Goal-setting is so important for sales success that I teach a whole ten-step goal setting system along with my sales system. I included it as a bonus chapter in my previous book *The System.* You can read that chapter to learn my whole goal-setting system. In this chapter I just want to make one key point as goal-setting applies to scripting:

Write your scripting goals down.

This is one of the biggest keys to successfully setting scripting goals, and it's so easy to do. All you need is a notebook and a few minutes. Reread Chapter 4 and use the exercise there to help you list the scripts you need to write, prioritize them, and pick some scripting goals.

Now let's talk about Strategy and Action. In terms of elevating your results from where you are right now to where you want to go, which one do you think is more important: Strategy or Action? I have asked this question to more than a hundred audiences, and I always get a split answer. Which one do you think is more important?

I believe strategy is more important by a wide margin. Yes, we absolutely must take action. But most successes come after having taking the *right* action, not after having taken any action.

As an example, consider Starbucks, which rapidly rose to dominance as a global brand. When Starbucks started, did the world need another coffee shop? Of course not. Did the world need a fancy coffee drink that cost $4 a cup? No. Yet Starbucks was able to go out and dominate markets on a global basis. Is this because they slapped together a strategy and went out and took massive action? Or, did they develop a superior strategy, and only then went out and took the massive action? Of course, it was the latter. Starbucks identified companies that had their target markets, then influenced these companies to serve Starbucks coffee. For instance, when Starbucks partnered Barnes & Noble, they got access to more than five hundred Barnes & Noble stores.

Let's look a little closer at a strategy. A strategy is like a completed puzzle. When you dissect a strategy, what you are left with are tactics. Tactics are like puzzle pieces. The strategy is the completed puzzle. Tactics woven together can form synergy. Synergy is doing more with less. Another way of describing synergy is: one plus one equals three. Sometimes one plus one equals thirty; sometimes one plus one equals three thousand; sometimes one plus one equals three million.

What I mean by this is that sometimes, when you combine tactics together—or companies together, or people together—something incredibly powerful happens. It's like when Ray Kroc met up with the McDonald brothers. Prior to meeting Kroc, the brothers had two successful McDonald's locations. When Kroc blended his real estate expansion and branding ideas with the burger concept that the McDonald brothers had come up with, McDonald's grew into a multi-billion dollar company. So when I say "one plus one equals three million," that's an example where Kroc, combined with the McDonald brothers, created something incredibly powerful.

In sales, I've found that combining the strategy of the Sales Mountain system with the strategy of scripting produces explosive results. To continue the puzzle analogy, following the steps in Sales Mountain and sales scripting is like looking at the picture on the puzzle box to help guide you as you put the puzzle together. Where it might take you days or weeks to complete a 1,000-piece jigsaw puzzle without the picture, if you start with the picture and use it to sort the pieces systematically, you can cut your time down to hours. In the same way, combining the strategies of sales systems and sales scripting can accelerate your business results faster than you thought possible.

A Real Life Example

Tactics woven together can form synergy. Let me share with you now some real-world examples of clients of mine that have applied this principle. And then I want to give you an example of how I have applied this principle.

The first client is Joey Azsterbaum. He's in the loan business. When I met Joey, he was an average loan officer. He had had months where he earned $10,000 each month. But he also was what I call a Dow Jones salesperson—his results were up and down, and thus not predicable. I started working with Joey on his tactics. First, I encouraged Joey to get a database and begin a systematic direct mail program. (I always encouraged clients to keep contacts in a database. My database is one of my most valuable business assets.) Joey has two types of customers: retail loan customers, and also real estate agents who bring him their buyers.

So Joey created two groups within his main database—a realtor group and a consumer group. He then developed a direct mail strategy for each. Later, he added outbound telemarketing. Then he hired an assistant. Then he put up a billboard in town that stayed up for about a year. Then Joey hired a sales person. Now Joey also did other things, but these were the key ones. He wove those tactics together. Tactics woven together can form synergy. Since implementing these tactics, Joey has earned more than $30,000 *in a month*, and for the last two years has been named Loan Officer of the Year at his company. He is one of the best students that I have ever had at applying the concept of GSA in his business.

As shown by Joey, tactics can come in all shapes and sizes. You can increase fees. You can expand your product line or service offerings. You can do more marketing. What new tactics might you introduce in your business? Start thinking about how you can weave them together to work synergistically.

Let me share with you a way that I have applied this concept in my business. [Strategy for Protege programs: combines public speaking, paid ads, affiliate marketing, landing page, automated webinar sells program, telemarketing to non-buyers, all of that combined. Automated webinar is scripted, ad, telemarketing, autoresponder, video on landing page, add link to Gold goldprotege.com]

http://goldprotege.com/

One of the ways that I help people is with sales scripting, and so I put up a one page website and the web address is:

www.freesalesscriptingreport.com

On this one page website, what's available is: a one-hour audio download, a word-for-word transcription (over fifteen pages) of that audio, and then there is a special report that reveals twenty-one different sales scripting techniques. The audio, the transcription, and the report are valued at over $100, and they are available for free at that website. You could go to that website right now and request those free tools.

So I put up that one page website and then when somebody goes to the website and requests the information, they enter their name, their phone number, and their email address, and that information automatically goes into my database. So that is a tactic.

And then we follow up with a phone call to the people that request the free report; that's a tactic. And the next thing we do is to develop the customer. The way we develop the customer is by offering them additional sales training products and services that would make sense for them.

So here is my projection of what's going to happen as a result of this strategy. Remember the strategy is the completed puzzle and the tactics are the puzzle pieces. The expected results from this website are 200 to 1000 leads per month at zero cost. That would generate around 5000 leads per year. From those 5000 leads I project that we would sell 500 DVDs at $49, 200 home study programs at $600, 100 boot camps at $1000 each, and twenty advance trainings at $5000 each. That would generate over $300,000 in revenue per year. In addition, those customers most likely will buy additional products and services in the future. We would also be generating referrals from those customers. Over the course of ten years this single idea is a $3-million idea—a great example of applied GSA.

Ideas Into Action

Todd Lay owns a paperless outsourced bookkeeping service. He had never received professional sales training before he started studying my system over six years ago. Todd began using scripts for handling objections, generating referrals, client reviews, marketing webinars, voice mails, follow-up email messages, and other applications. Since implementing my methods, Todd has doubled the size of his database to over 2,857 contacts and tripled his revenue to over $20,000 a month. Todd writes, "Eric's training and influence has had a profound impact on my life and my business. Around the time I had been introduced to Eric, I was about at my lowest of lows financially ever. My wife and I were in the midst of losing our home of over ten years, our third child was on the way, we had filed for bankruptcy, and were down to one car for a soon-to-be a family of five...There was NO PLAN B, and I was not going to miss that Sales Scripting Bootcamp in San Francisco, California. So with my wife over nine months pregnant (due any day), and down to one car, I did the unthinkable at that time...I had my wife drop me off at the local Amtrak train station, then got on BART to the SFO Airport, then took the hotel shuttle from the airport to where Eric was hosting his Sales Scripting Bootcamp. It took over 4 hours to finally get there instead of a 90-minute car ride...I was committed. During that session I focused on writing out my-much needed scripts for my business...Over the last couple of years my wife and I have become homeowners again, I've surprised my wife with a new SUV on Christmas day (the kids no longer complain of being squished in the car), one year I surprised her with a delivery of new living room furniture. My biggest suggestion is to 'stay in the conversation' with Eric and 'work at the speed of instruction' as he says often."

To apply the GSA strategy to scripting, I invite you to commit to three actions that will have a big impact on your results:

> First, commit to writing down your scripting goals. Use the strategy outlined in Chapter 4 to decide which scripts you need to prioritize and which one is most important to complete first.
>
> Second, commit to writing down your scripts, one script at a time.
>
> Third, take action on writing your scripts. The next few chapters will focus on how to do this.

Key Points Review

- The concept of GSA is based on billionaire J. Paul Getty's teaching that all you need to do to achieve anything in life is to ask yourself what you want, then develop the strategy to achieve it, then take massive action on a daily basis.

- For the Goal part of GSA, write your scripting goals down.

- Strategy plays a bigger role in elevating your results than Action. Combining the strategy of sales systems with the strategy of sales scripting can multiply your results.

- Taking action means applying tactics that turn your strategies into results.

- One of the best strategies you can put into action to achieve business results is writing down your sales scripts. You can get more help with your sales scripts by visiting: **http://goldprotege.com/**

PART III

PUTTING SCRIPTING INTO ACTION

In the previous chapters, we've laid the foundation for you to put sales scripting into action. In Part I, we instilled the mindset you need to overcome resistance to scripting and get past scriptwriter's block. Part II mapped out a step-by-step scripting strategy and gave you sample scripts you can use to implement this strategy. Now it's time to put that strategy into action. The following chapters will focus on putting the scriptwriting skills you've learned into practice putting your scripts to work making more sales. We'll cover:

- Getting your scripts written
- Rehearsing your scripts
- Delivering your scripts
- How to sound spontaneous during your presentations

Putting these chapters into action will take you from strategy to sales.

Chapter 15

Getting Your Scripts Written

Procrastination is the enemy of action. For many people, one of the biggest barriers to scriptwriting is simply getting started with actually writing your scripts. This can be a challenge even for me at times. It took me nearly ten years to finish my first book before I finally made a commitment to get it done. Once I made that commitment, the book was completed within six months. Once you get into action, you gain momentum, and finishing your scripts becomes easier. In this chapter we'll focus on getting the ball rolling.

Write Down Your Scripting Goals

In the last chapter on GSA, I emphasized the importance of writing down your scripting goals. This is the first step towards getting into action. Once you write down your goals, you've accomplished several things.

First, you've started the writing process. You are now in action.

Second, you've put your goals into visible form. You can now see what you're working towards.

Third, you've declared your intent. You are now holding yourself accountable.

If you haven't done so already, go back to Chapter 4 and write down your scripting goals. List the scripts you need written. Prioritize them. Pick one to write first. Then come back to this chapter and take the next step.

Schedule Scriptwriting Time

Back in Chapter 2, when I was talking about breaking through scriptwriter's block, I stressed the importance of scheduling scriptwriting time. I introduced the distinction that what doesn't get scheduled doesn't get done. I recommended that you'll find it easier to commit to a definite block of time if you limit the amount of writing time you schedule to something you find manageable. I suggested that using a timer to schedule writing blocks of ten to thirty minutes can help you write in intense bursts while giving you a chance to recover your energy.

I recommend that you combine these tips with using a calendar tool to schedule writing time. Which tool you use is up to you. You can use a notebook, a desktop calendar, a spreadsheet program such as Excel, a calendar program such as Outlook, or a smartphone calendar app such as Apple's Calendar. Whatever tool you use, the main point is to block out a set writing time to work on your script.

I help my students put this strategy into practice in a couple ways. One way is offering weekly scriptwriting classes, which sometimes include in-class exercise time devoted to applying specific scripting techniques covered in that lesson. Between classes students get homework assignments which they can share with me and their classmates. I also include scriptwriting time in longer, more intense virtual workshops. During these workshops I share scriptwriting techniques, then give my students some time to apply the information to their own scripts, and follow up by providing some review time where participants' scripts can receive feedback from me, my coaching team, and fellow students. To learn more about the scriptwriting opportunities I offer, visit the page for my Gold Protege Program:

http://goldprotege.com/

Track Your Progress

To make your scheduling effective, it's important to follow up by tracking your progress. As you complete each of your scripts and sections of your scripts, use paper or software to mark progress on a checklist based on your laundry list. This way you can see your progress towards completing your scripts, which will help motivate you. It will also help keep you focused on taking the next step, and it will let you see when each script is complete so you can move on to the next one.

Ideas Into Action

James Pereira was first introduced to sales scripting in 1994 as a Product Manager for a Pharmaceutical Multi-national Company in Malaysia. James writes:

> As the marketing person responsible for my range of products, I had to create sales scripts for the core products in my portfolio. These scripts included then entire presentation script from the moment the sales rep entered the doctor's door until the close.
>
> I also created scripts for handling customer responses which included Questions, Misunderstandings and Objections.
>
> This was a company wide exercise.
>
> The initial impact was of course resistance from the entire sales force—the sales managers and sales reps. However after going through the process, the sales team embraced the idea of sales scripts.
>
> In my field work with the sales reps, I could see how comfortable the reps were in their sales presentations and confidence when handling objections. We convinced customers to switch to our products much more easily than in the past before sales scripting was introduced.
>
> When I moved to 2 other companies, I introduced sales scripting to those as well and the same reactions from the sales teams played out and the same results were obtained in the field eventually.
>
> Early June 2015, I conducted a Selling Skills training session with another company and I introduced sales scripting to them too. It was a 2 day program and they all had sore fingers at the end of the 2nd day, as they had never written so much for so long. But they were all more confident that they could present more smoothly and handle customer responses easily.

The moral of these stories is that sales scripting is a fundamental sales technique that is relevant even in the 21st Century. Secondly, sales scripting works in Asia as well as for customers in the scientific field (healthcare professionals in this case).

Remember, action is the number one key ingredient to all success and all achievement. Only by taking action on scripting will you achieve massive results. Remember:

The universe rewards people who take action differently than those who don't.

To start taking action on the scriptwriting techniques in this book, go to the Success Journal at the end of the book where you've been recording the best ideas you've been learning as you've been reading. (Remember I told you to do that back in the Introduction?) Pick the two best ideas you've learned and focus on putting those into action first.

After you've made some progress implementing those ideas, pick another one to work on. Treat this as a workbook to study and apply, not just something you read once. The value you get out of this book will depend on what you put into applying it. I can teach you everything I know about sales, but it's up to you to take action. I encourage you to read this book at least seven times to really absorb the ideas in it on a deeper level. This is part of staying in the conversation.

Key Points Review

- Write down your scripting goals.
- Schedule scripting time.
- Track your progress.

Chapter 16

Rehearsal

Whenever I give a sales speech, I think of it like a professional baseball player taking batting practice. Ted Williams, considered one of the greatest hitters of all time with a career .344 batting average, achieved his success for a number of reasons, one of which was his dedication to batting practice. From the age of about six, Williams would go to a local baseball park and practice from morning until the time the park turned the lights off. Witnesses described him swinging until his fingers were blistered and blood was dripping down his wrists, even after he had splintered bats and wore the hide off balls. Williams continued this habit into his major league career, showing up first for practice and asking for used balls so he could do extra batting after supper. When Ted Williams stepped up to the plate, his swing had been rehearsed for literally tens of thousands of hours. And the hard work showed. Some observers said watching him swing a bat was like watching ballet. To the untrained eye, Williams' swing looked totally natural, like he was born swinging a bat. Only those who knew him knew how much rehearsal had gone into developing that swing.

Every great sales representative or public speaker also puts in many hours of rehearsal. I've delivered my own key sales talks multiple times a week for decades, and I've seen speakers like Dante Perano, Tony Robbins, and Les Brown give the same speeches over and over again. For example, over the past three decades, Tony Robbins has delivered his signature fire walk seminar to over 2 million people. Rehearsal is vital to delivering your sales scripts effectively. In this chapter I'm going to give you four ways to improve the quality of your rehearsals and translate the results into better presentations and more sales.

Scheduling

My first tip is to schedule rehearsal time into your regular routine. I practice each major presentation I deliver, often more than once. For me this is a habit, but the reason it's a habit is because I make it a regular practice. The way to make it a regular practice is to schedule a regular practice time.

One way I help my students schedule regular script rehearsal times is by offering training calls for this purpose. Higher levels of my sales training program include "role play" conference calls where my trainers deliver their sales scripts over the phone to other trainers. Their listeners act out the role of prospects, and they also provide feedback. By holding role play calls regularly, I help my trainers build regular rehearsal time into their schedules.

Sometimes you will not have much time to rehearse before a presentation. This could be because you got busy doing something else, or it could be because the presentation got scheduled at the last minute. In this case, try to at least schedule time to review the outline of your script and key sections such as your close. This will make a big difference to your performance and results even when you don't have time to schedule a full rehearsal.

Memorizing

Memorization is an important part of rehearsal. When you've put in time memorizing your scripts, they come to your mind more quickly and they flow more smoothly. This takes away the stress of trying to remember your script, so that instead of focusing on finding the right words, you can focus on your prospect. In this way, memorization actually makes you sound more spontaneous.

Ideally you should be able to remember your entire script, even if you don't end up reciting it word for word. However there are some parts of your script that are more essential to your sales results than others, and you should take special care to memorize these.

The first thing it's important to memorize is the structure of your script. This includes your outline as well as the transitions between the major sections of your script. Memorizing your outline helps keep you on track so you know where you are in Sales Mountain at any point in your presentation, telling you what step you should be focusing on and what comes next. Memorizing transitions helps cue your memory when it's time to shift into the next section of your script. For instance, if you can remember the opening words of your close, it can trigger your memory of your whole close.

You should memorize the most important key points of your script word for word. Key points it pays to memorize word for word include:

- Your close, which is the most important item
- Key supporting components of your close, such as supporting details about how to take action on your call to action
- Your introduction, which is important for getting your memory in the right state of mind to remember the rest of your script
- Probing questions
- Lists of key points, such as lists of benefits
- Most common objections and answers to them

When memorizing parts of your script, here are a few memory tips to help you:

- Write your scripts down to help engrain them in your memory
- Number the sections of your outline and any lists in your script (such as lists of probing questions, benefits, or objections) so you can refer back to your numbering to remember where you are
- Review your written scripts both silently and aloud
- Record your scripts, listen to the recordings, and repeat what you hear
- Create slideshows to help you see and remember your major scripts
- Practice delivering your scripts to others to reinforce your memory

Applying these memorization tips will make it easier for you to remember your scripts so you can deliver them with less anxiety and get better results.

Practicing

When practicing your scripts, you will get the best results from your practice if you follow a systematic, step-by-step process. I recommend a series of steps which supports the memorization tips I just mentioned in the previous section and builds on them:

1. Write your scripts down
2. Review your scripts silently
3. Read your scripts aloud and record what you read
4. Review your recordings silently (with visual aids added if you choose to create a slideshow)
5. Review your recordings, repeating what you hear aloud
6. Rehearse your script by delivering it to another person, who can offer objections for you to handle if the script calls for it
7. Deliver your script to live audiences, recording them when possible
8. Review your recordings of your live presentations

Following these steps will both improve your memorization of your scripts and build your confidence and your ability to adapt your scripts to live situations.

Improving

One reason I recommended recording your script rehearsal sessions and live presentations was so you can review your recordings in order to make improvements. Making improvements to your presentation is related to the process of revising, improving, and updating your scripts discussed in Chapter 10, but it focuses more specifically on improving your delivery.

I'll talk more about delivery and what it consists of in the next chapter. For now, I'll mention a few general things you can listen for as you review your presentation, as well as what you can watch for if you recorded a video of your presentation:

- How does my tone of voice sound?
- Am I audible and clear?
- Do I sound confident?

- Does my voice vary in volume, pace, and emotional intensity?
- How is my body language? Check your eye movements, posture, gestures, and movements on stage.
- Is my message strong?
- Did I effectively build trust and rapport with interesting stories or humor?
- Did I ask good questions?
- Did I sound enthusiastic when conveying benefits?
- Did I sound persuasive when delivering my close?
- Did I sound convincing when answering objections?

Focus on improving one element of your presentation at a time. Over time, the improvements will add up, and your overall impact will improve.

Exercise

Schedule a time to rehearse one of your high-priority scripts. Record yourself, review your recording, and take notes on one to three things you could improve. Then rehearse and record your script again, focusing on your desired improvements.

Ideas Into Action

When Rhonda Sher met me she had never been trained in how to create a great sales script. She had been successful by relying on her charisma versus preparing her sales presentation in advance. Rhonda attended one of my public speaking courses. In the course, everyone was required to learn the same script and present a portion of it each day in class. The students presented a portion of the script for the first time on Day 2. When it was Rhonda's turn, she really struggled because she hadn't spent much time preparing. When Rhonda returned to class on Day 3, she struggled again because she hadn't prepared much again. Then it hit her how important learning the script was. She did great on Day 4 because she really practiced her script. She then decided that she would take this realization back with her and apply it to her sales calls. Rhonda sells on conference calls. With my help she put together a winning script. Prior to using the script she would do $100-$200 in sales per conference call. On the very first call where she used the script, she did $2,500 in sales! Rhonda always wanted to purchase a car for all cash from the profits from her business. Within six months of embracing sales scripting, she purchased a $48,000 car with all cash! Rhonda has used her scripting skills for the last ten years, making her hundreds of thousands of additional dollars in income!

Key Points Review

- Schedule rehearsal time.

- Memorize your outline, transitions, and the key parts of your script, especially your close.

- Practice step-by-step by yourself and with others.

- As you practice, make improvements by adjusting one piece at a time.

Chapter 17

Delivery

The legendary ancient Roman speaker Cicero considered delivery to be the biggest difference between an average speaker and a great speaker. What makes a powerful public speaker like John F. Kennedy, Ronald Reagan, Martin Luther King, or Les Brown stand out above the crowd is not just what they say, but the way they say it. Imagine how different Darth Vader's lines would have sounded if he stuttered like Elmer Fudd. As this illustrates, you could put the exact same lines in two different speakers' mouths and get two totally different effects. This highlights the importance of delivery. In this chapter I'm going to describe some of the keys to improving your delivery.

Voice

Your voice is the most important component of your delivery, and using it effectively revolves around managing your tone of voice. Some speakers use the same pitch and pacing throughout their speech, which makes them drone like a lecturer. Other speakers overcompensate for this by emphasizing every word, which comes across like constant shouting, and has the effect of desensitizing the audience's ear: you can't emphasize anything if you emphasize everything.

The happy medium is to use a standard tone of voice which you can vary as needed. Use your normal speaking tone for most of your speech. Vary your pitch and pacing when you need to emphasize something. You can raise the volume or sink to a whisper. You can speed up or slow down. Change your pitch and pace to let your audience know when you're highlighting something important.

Eyes

In situations where your audience can see you (which is not always the case), your eyes have the second-biggest impact on your delivery, after your voice. Your eyes convey your emotions. They also serve as your visual connection with your audience. Use your eyes to communicate the emotional tone you want to convey when delivering a part of your script. You can also use your eyes to convey grammatical intent, such as whether you're asking a question, making a statement, or inviting action.

Posture

Posture is another important element of delivery. Your posture can affect your overall delivery because it impacts your breathing, which in turn influences your voice. Leaning over, slouching, or tensing your shoulders tends to make your breathing more shallow, which affects your volume and pacing. Standing up straight and relaxing your shoulders will deepen your breathing and the quality of your annunciation.

Standing up straight also affects your visual appearance. Hunching over makes you look smaller and less confident, weakening your authority and your ability to maintain trust and rapport. Straightening up gives you a stronger visual presence.

Gestures

Gestures can also enhance your delivery. Use hand motions to dramatize the rhythms of your speech and to punctuate key lines. However, unless you're a natural at talking with your hands, be careful not to overdo it, or you run the risk of diluting the effect. Save your big gestures for your most important lines.

Foot gestures should be used even more sparingly. Foot actions such as stomping carry a lot of emotional impact and should be used as judiciously as exclamation points.

Position

Where you stand on stage can also influence your delivery. As a rule, stay in one spot unless you have a specific reason for moving. Reasons for changing position include stressing a specific part of your speech, giving a section a different emotional tone than the rest of your talk, or acting out dialogue between two imaginary parties standing in different locations.

Improving Your Delivery

You can work on improving your delivery in any of the above areas. For best results, I suggest working on improving one thing at a time. Ideally, record a video of yourself giving a talk so you can see how you do in each area. Pick one area that would most improve your delivery and work on that first.

Exercise

Record your next rehearsal or speech on audio or video. Review the recording with the tips from this chapter in mind. Pick one thing you could improve upon. Try to improve that thing in your next talk, and record that one to see how you did.

Ideas Into Action

Yoram Baltinester works in the seminar and training business delivering programs and workshops on sales, business success, and personal development. Before he began training with me, he had never received any professional sales training. Yoram writes, "Since I started to use sales scripting I found that I have an easier time booking more business. I do not have to think and reinvent the wheel every time I deliver a program or have a sales discussion with a potential buyer. I know what phrases and words to use to lead them to buy, make them feel great about it, and point to the benefits of the program that correspond to the needs that they have. So I use them over and over again. Consistent use of the scripts produces a consistent sales result, and allows me to improve them over time to get even better results. So initially I used the scripting techniques in another business that I owned and I was able to increase that business to the point that I successfully sold it. Now I am using the same techniques in my current business to grow it and it has brought me from a complete beginner in the month of August 2013 to becoming the #3 worldwide income earner in 2013, and the #2 for 2014."

Key Points Review

- ■ Delivery separates average speakers from great speakers.

- ■ Delivery is influenced by your voice, eyes, posture, gestures, and position.

- ■ To improve your delivery, work on improving one component at a time.

Chapter 18

From Scripting
to Spontaneity

One of the most famous and successful public speeches of all time was Martin Luther King's "I Have a Dream" speech. If you watch a video of King delivering the speech, you're impressed by the sincere emotion he projects, which amplifies the speech's power. It comes across as very spontaneous. And it was, but this did not mean King had not rehearsed.

King had actually spent a great deal of time in preparation. He had given the "I Have a Dream" section of his speech several times before. In fact, his adviser Wyatt Walker had recommended not including that section of the speech, arguing "You've used it too many times already."

King spent the night before the speech editing a first draft that had been written by his lawyer Clarence Jones. Jones later said King was up reworking the speech until 4 a.m. He had crossed out some words as many as four times, like he was composing a poem. When he finally gave his aides the text of the speech to distribute, the "I Have a Dream" section was not in the final draft.

After King got on stage and neared the end of his prepared speech, he sensed it was not going over as powerfully as he had hoped. At that moment, gospel singer Mahalia Jackson, who had heard King speak before, called out, "Tell 'em about the dream, Martin!"

At that moment, King grabbed the podium and set aside his prepared text. At that moment, the speech changed. Jones later recalled, "When he was reading from his text, he stood like a lecturer. . .But from the moment he set that text aside, he took on the stance of a Baptist preacher." Jones turned to the person standing next to him and said: "Those people don't know it, but they're about to go to church."

As King's speech illustrates, a rehearsed speech can still be very spontaneous if you know how to adjust to the occasion. Early in the book I mentioned that one reason people avoid scripting is because they fear sounding rehearsed. In this chapter I'll share some tips to help overcome this fear.

Change Your State

One thing you probably noticed in Jones' recollection of King's speech is how King's stance suddenly changed when he shifted from lecturing into preaching. In psychology, this is known as a change in state. A change in state is a change in both your body posture and physiology and in your emotional and mental state.

For example, if you're depressed, you will tend to do things such as look down, slump your shoulders, and breathe shallowly. If you change these components of your physical state, it can often change your emotional state as well. To illustrate, imagine how difficult it would be to remain in a depressed physical state while doing jumping jacks or jogging. Your body can't easily do these things and remain depressed at the same time.

To take advantage of this phenomenon, one trick public speakers use is to practice a ritual to get into a good emotional state before they speak. To practice this, first you create the state by getting into the right mood, adjusting components of your physical, emotional, and mental state. These include your posture, gestures, breathing, voice, and eye movements. Another component is your internal feelings, such as which muscles feel tight or loose. A third piece is internal experiences such as what images you're picturing and what you're saying to yourself in your mind. Finally, what you say aloud can influence how you feel.

After adjusting all these elements to create your state, you create what is called a "trigger" to help you get into the right mood on cue. A trigger is a cue such as a physical action (like clenching your fist), a key word or phrase ("SHAZAM!"), or an image you picture to remind yourself of the state you want to get into. Practice associating your trigger with your desired speaking state by getting yourself into the state and then performing whatever action you've selected to activate the trigger. You can check how effectively you've conditioned the trigger by changing your state, doing something else for a while, and then tripping the trigger again to see if it alters your state as intended. You will usually need to practice multiple times to get the trigger to stick. Over time, it will become instinctive. You can also create alternate triggers to achieve the same state.

Practice triggering your state before your speeches. Then get in the habit of using your trigger when you start speaking. This can add emotional vitality and spontaneity to your speaking.

Engage Your Audience

Another way to add spontaneity is by actively engaging your audience. If you're just reading your rehearsed speech without interacting with the people hearing it, you are essentially speaking to yourself, and you will lack an emotional connection with your audience. Being aware of your audience and how you're interacting with them can make your speech more engaging. There are a few methods you can use to achieve this.

One important technique, discussed in the previous chapter on delivery, is vocal variation. If you use the same tone throughout your speech, your audience will tend to become too relaxed, bored, or annoyed. Use vocal variation to lead your audience through different emotional states, allowing your tone and pacing to rise and fall in rhythms that keep your audience auditorily engaged.

Asking questions is another way to get your audience involved. When you ask a question, your listener's natural instinct is to think about the question and respond in their head or out loud. This keeps your audience paying attention. In some situations you can ask questions but your audience won't necessarily have an opportunity to answer aloud. In other cases you can talk with your audience. I often ask questions of live audiences. I've also used this technique over the phone and through virtual media such as webinars and Facebook.

If your audience can see you, eye contact is extremely important. Making eye contact with members of your audience is the best way to emotionally engage them. The eye movements you make have the biggest impact on the emotions you convey. If you need help maintaining eye contact, one technique some speakers use is picking out several audience members at key checkpoints in the room to look at periodically. You can pick out one member in the middle, one on the right, and one on the left. Cycle through your selected audience members periodically to keep your eyes emotionally engaged with your audience.

If your audience can see you or a screen you have control over, another technique you can use is visual aids. Visual aids help you control what your audience is looking at. They can also help make the information you present easier to visualize, understand, and relate to emotionally. You can use visual aids in live presentations if you have props or A/V equipment. You can also use them in virtual environments if you can refer your audience to a webpage or webinar screenshot they can look at while you're talking. If you plan to use visual aids, make sure you plan them ahead of time. Collect any visual aids you plan to use, note where to introduce them in your script, and test any technology you'll be using to make sure it works.

Engage Your Topic

A third method of keeping your speeches spontaneous is staying engaged with your topic. If you're just saying words without thinking about what you're saying, your words will sound empty. Keeping your mind focused on your topic will bring your words alive. There are a few ways you can achieve this.

One thing that can help keep you focused on the content of your talk is visualizing what you're talking about. For instance, if you're telling a story, imagine yourself or other characters in the story, and picture the setting.

You can also act out your speech. Some speakers move around stage to deliver different parts of their speech from different positions. Gestures also help dramatize your speech. If you use movements and gestures, make sure they match your words. Don't just move for the sake of moving, but make your movements meaningful. Save your most dramatic movements for the key points in your talk.

A third way to engage your topic is verbalizing internal questions and dialogue that arise spontaneously in response to your words. For instance, you might ask a question aloud about something you just said, and let your audience hear your answer. You can also act out different people exchanging ideas or arguing.

Exercise

The next time you deliver a speech, apply one of the ideas from this chapter. You might decide to practice triggering the emotional state you want before your speech. You can also practice engaging your audience using verbal variation, questions, eye contact, or visual aids. Or you can decide to practice one of the techniques for engaging your topic. Work on one of the ideas from this chapter at a time. Incorporate more of this chapter's techniques as you deliver more speeches.

Ideas Into Action

Walter Kaminski works in financial services as a financial coach and advisor. He had never received professional sales training before he began training with me in January 2010. Walter doubled his assets in his first year he started training with me, and since then he has tripled his income. Walter writes, "By working with Eric, I have developed the confidence to handle any situation with ease. He has made selling become effortless and fun. I really enjoy what I do and now I have a way to communicate that to my clients, prospects and anyone I want to persuade or influence. Eric has also been instrumental in expanding my comfort zones so I can continually look for ways to improve in all areas of my life."

Key Points Review

- Get in the right emotional mood before speaking by practicing using triggers to adjust your physical, emotional, and mental state.

- Engage your audience by using techniques such as vocal variation, questions, eye contact, and visual aids.

- Engage your topic by visualizing what you're talking about, acting it out, and verbalizing internal questions and dialogue.

Conclusion

I'd like to conclude by acknowledging you for finishing this book. Congratulations! I'd love to hear from you. Send an email to my private email address:

wins@ericlofholm.com.

Let me know that you finished the book, and share with me one idea that you learned that was helpful.

PART IV

BONUS MATERIAL

Bonus Chapter #1

77 Sales Scripting Techniques

In this bonus chapter I'm going to share 77 sales scripting techniques I've used successfully over the course of my sales career. Use them individually or in combination to help you write your scripts. Refer to this bonus chapter when you're brainstorming for script ideas.

General Scripting Techniques

1. Future Pace

This technique is letting the prospect know how they are going to experience something in the future. For example, if I were selling a car I might tell a prospect, "When you pull into the driveway in your new car you are going to be excited knowing the neighbors are going to view you as a success." In this example, I future pace the prospect about how they are going to feel when they drive into the driveway. This is a great technique to use to help prospects avoid buyer's remorse.

2. Connect the Known to the Unknown

Part of selling is education. One way to educate someone is to connect something they know to something they don't know. Below is an example of this.

Front of the room, telemarketing, or face-to-face script

I would like to talk with you about the importance of structure. Often times, you can accomplish the results you are seeking effortlessly by changing your structure.

How many of you at one point in your life have owned a VCR? You have either had one or currently have one, by a show of hands? [Lead the audience by raising your hand.]

Tell me if you can relate with this. There were a lot of shows that you would have liked to record but didn't because either [mind reading technique]:

> You never could get the light for the clock to stop flashing.
> It was a hassle to program your VCR.
> You would forget.
> It was a difficult to locate a blank VCR tape.

How many of you can relate with that? [Let them agree.]

A VCR is a structure. It is a structure that allows you to record a TV program.

I recently purchased a DVR. If you are not familiar with it is a digital VCR. How many of you have a DVR? [This builds rapport with the audience; wait for response]. Aren't they great? [creates agreement undeniable truth] A DVR is a structure as well. Its purpose, just like the VCR, is to record a TV program. The benefit of the DVR is you can record an entire series with the touch of a few buttons on your remote control. For example if you want to record the entire series of Survivor you can do it in less than a minute. You can even set up the recording while you are watching TV.

When I used to have my VCR I recorded 10 TV programs in 10 years. With my new DVR I regularly record 10 programs in a week! I am recording 500 times more shows than I was with the VCR. Is this because I am more motivated? [Let them respond.]

Is it because I have more discipline or will power? [Let them respond.]

The reason I am producing this result is because I changed structures. Think about how you can apply this concept in your business. What structures can you change to grow your business?

3. Nested Story

A nested story is a story inside of a story. The movie *Titanic* is a nested story. It begins with an old woman. She then shares the story of her as a young woman. The story about her as a young woman is a story inside of a story. This is a powerful technique to deepen your influence with the prospect.

4. Contrast

This is a technique to build value in your product or service. Low-priced cars use this technique. Here is an example:

The Honda Accord is similar to the BMW Sedan except you don't have to put high octane fuel in it and it is one-third of the price.

5. Charts and Graphs

Charts and graphs can be very persuasive. Look for ways to use these visual selling tools in your presentation.

6. Define New Words that You Use

Often times it is necessary to use words in your presentation that the prospect is not familiar with. Anytime you introduce a new word make sure you define the word.

7. Flattery

Flattery is one of the most persuasive scripting techniques. Tell people how nice their smile is, how their new haircut looks great, how nice their house looks. Flattery is a great way to build rapport.

8. Direct Command

Human beings respond to direct commands. Look for ways to use direct commands in your presentation.

9. Storytelling

Storytelling is one of the most powerful scripting techniques. Storytelling is fun, easy and persuasive.

You can use story scripts throughout the sales process.

When you think about scripting, you want to think about the moment you first get the lead to the last communication you are going to have with the prospect. This time frame might span 20 years.

Storytelling can be used:

- During lead generation
- When setting the appointment
- When the prospect tries to cancel the appointment
- Throughout the appointment
- When handling objections
- During the close
- When asking for referrals
- From the front of the room
- On a conference call

Different types of stories you can tell

- Your story
- Your client's story
- Your company story
- Stories from the media
- Tell stories people can relate with.

Here is a great script:

> That reminds me of a client I recently worked with. He had the same concern you did...

Or

> Maybe you can relate with this. One of my clients...

Stories:

- Create rapport
- Suspend time
- Influence on a subconscious level

- Bring benefits to life
- Reduce and/or eliminate objections
  - Induce a trancelike state
  - You want to use stories strategically during your presentation to further influence, build rapport, reduce objections, or all three.
- Create a file to keep track of the stories you could tell during your sales presentation.

Here is a way to use a story in a script. You can tell a success story that educates the prospect on the result you can produce. It has been said many times that prospects buy you. This is not true. Prospects buy benefits. They are buying a result. One of the most persuasive ways to communicate the result you can deliver is to share a success story of someone in a similar situation. Here is a script that I used to pick up a recent client, I told a story of a client that was similar to him: This story helped educate him on how I could help him.

> Mrs. X came to me to see if I could help her telemarketing team increase their results. I told her that I absolutely could help her. I asked her about her team … about where they were strong and where they were weak. I also asked her what she thought they were capable of in terms of monthly sales. I told her the initial investment would be $5,000. I would write several scripts for that fee that would more than pay for the $5,000 investment. She could then take a small percentage of the profits and reinvest in more scripting and consulting work.
>
> Once she made the initial investment she would never need to come out of pocket ever again. Over time everything I told her happened. Her team went from $100,000 in sales per month to over a $300,000 in sales per month. I think I could do something similar with your team.

10. Repeated "Yes" Technique

These are statements throughout the presentation where the prospect will say yes.

11. Helping Scripts

People love to help. Close the prospect by asking them for their help.

> Example: Can you do me a favor?
>
> Example: Can you help me out?
>
> Example: I need your help. (This is a direct command)

Helping scripts are especially persuasive if you are in rapport with the prospect and it is a reasonable request at a reasonable time.

12. Reasonable Request at a Reasonable Time

Many times salespeople get a "no" in a presentation because they asked for something at the wrong time. Timing is very important.

13. Progressively More Demanding

This is a great technique when you are requesting something from someone and you are not getting what you want. Let's say you are at a restaurant and they didn't prepare your food properly.

The first step could be a simple request that they redo your order. If you don't get the answer you are looking for you can get a little more demanding. Continue to get more demanding until you get the result you are looking for.

14. Preframe

Let the prospect know in advance what is going to happen. Here is an example of preframing for referrals:

> As you probably know I work with referrals. After you have received value from me I would like to ask you for referrals. Would that be okay?

In this example I didn't ask for referrals now. I preframed the prospect that once they have received value I will be asking for referrals.

15. Trigger Phrase "Imagine"

The word "imagine" is a very powerful word. You are giving the prospect a direct command to imagine. Follow the phrase imagine by focusing the prospect's attention on some key benefits of your product or service. Here is an example:

> Imagine you are now 65 years old. Because you got started today with your retirement plan you now have all the money you need to live the life you want. How would that feel?

16. Social Proof

This is third party endorsement: someone other than you saying that you, your company, or your product and service are great. When someone else endorses you, you can achieve a level of influence that you can't create on your own.

17. Testimonials

Testimonials are a form of social proof. Nothing sells like success. The best testimonials provide specific results the customer has received from your product or service.

Here is an example of a bad testimonial:

> "Eric's program is great—John Smith."

Here is an example of a great testimonial:

> Before I met Eric my best income month ever was around $10,000. Six months after I joined Eric's program my income soared to over $30,000 using Eric's ideas. Not only has my income increased but so has my time with my family. Because my income has increased I have been able to take family vacations in the last 12 months. That is more vacations than I have taken in the last 5 years combined. If you are looking for proven ideas that will increase your sales Eric can help you.
>
> Joey Aszterbaum
> 6951 285 1012
> www.joeyloans.com

In a front-of-the-room presentation you can show a picture of the person providing testimonial, show a magazine article, or show a testimonial letter.

18. Endorsements

A great way to add influence to your script is to mention people or companies that endorse you. In a front-of-the-room presentation you can show a picture of the person providing the endorsement, show a magazine article, or show an endorsement letter.

19. Borrow Other People's Scripts

Human beings respond in predictable ways. You can use the same scripts that others use and produce a similar result. Not all scripts work for all people. If you are more passive and you are using a script written by someone who has a dominant personality, it may not work for you.

20. Mind Reading Technique

This is a powerful way to create rapport with a person or group. It lets them know you understand them. The technique is to tell them what they are thinking before they tell you.

21. Undeniable Truth

You are reading this sentence right now. "You are in my scripting teleseminar." "You live in America or Canada." "You will benefit from your completed sales script." These are all undeniable truths. These act as pacing statements to build rapport. They also create harmony with the prospect.

22. Leading Language

This is where you leave out the phrase in the sentence so the prospect says the phrase for you. There is a different level of influence when the prospect says the phrase versus you saying it.

An example of leading language is when the lead singer in a concert turns the microphone towards the audience letting them know to sing the words to the song. Here is a script example:

> "If you do what a millionaire does, you will get what a millionaire has. If you invest your money where millionaires currently have their money invested, what would you become?"

> The prospect will say, "a millionaire."

Close Techniques

23. Takeaway

This is where you offer the prospect a deal and then you take the deal away. You demand action or the deal is off.

- The special is good until 5:00 today.
- I need an answer now or the price I quoted you will no longer be good.
- I am looking at 2 houses. I need an answer now or I am going to go with the other house.

24. Alternate of Choice

This is where you give the prospect 2 or more choices where both choices are a yes.

- Would you like the blue one or the red one?
- You can pay with Visa or MasterCard. Which would work best for you?
- I have an opening on Thursday at 4 or Friday at 4. Which would you prefer?

25. Ask

Simply ask the prospect to move forward.

26. "How Do You Feel?" Close

This is a very soft close. Simply ask the prospect how they feel about setting an appointment, moving forward with the listing, getting started today, the insurance policy you offered them, etc.

27. Assumption Close

This is where you don't ask the prospect if they would like to move forward. You assume they are. You could ask them:

- Where would you like your desk delivered?
- What day would you like me to start?
- Which credit card will you be using today?
- Sign here please.
- How many months are you going to start off with?

28. Reduce the Risk

This is where you change the offer that is on the table by removing some of the risk for the prospect. For example if you were asking them to purchase six months of service you might reduce the risk by allowing them to purchase only three months.

29. Bonus

Offer a bonus as an incentive for taking action now. People will buy from you today if you give them a reason to buy from you today. Marriott recently offered me 60,000 Marriott points if I purchased from them this month. Think about bonuses you could offer your customers.

30. Reduce It to the Ridiculous

Some products and services seem expensive when you look solely at the price. Oftentimes the prospect hasn't thought about how long they will enjoy the benefits of the product or service when evaluating price. Pointing this out to them helps them see the value you are offering.

Here is an example: "The price of the program is $299. It is a yearlong program. That makes your investment less then $25 per month or less than a $1 per day. You will be able to enjoy the benefits of the program for the next 10 years. That makes the program less than $30 per year. Would you agree $30 per year would be a great investment to increase your income over $10,000 per year?"

31. "Would You Feel Comfortable?" Close

This is a very soft way of closing. Simply say, "Would you feel comfortable moving forward today?" Then be silent.

32. Trial Close

The trial close is where you get a minor agreement from the prospect. They are saying yes that takes they close to the sale.

33. Timing

Closing has timing to it. Closing is similar to poker. Sometimes in poker you bet a certain way to influence what the other players think you have. In some cases you will bluff, placing a large wager in hopes the other players fold.

34. Ask for the Order and Be Silent

Part of the language of influence is silence. After you ask for the order be silent. I close every one-on-one sale using this technique.

Identify Customer Needs Techniques

35. Buyer Fingerprint

Human beings make buying decisions in patterns. We each have our own fingerprint. The buyer fingerprint is the pattern of how the prospect makes buying decisions.

36. Probing Questions

The easiest way to persuade or influence someone is to find out what they want and give it to them. The way to find out what they want is by asking questions.

37. Probing Statements

These are statements where the prospect shares more information with you. An example is "Tell me more about that."

38. Trial Close Based on Probing Question Answers

When the prospect answers a question in some cases there is an opportunity for you to trial close. For example:

- How much do you have in your budget?
- $4,000.
- If we can deliver a solution within your budget would you be ready to move forward?
- Do they pay with cash or credit?
- Does anyone else help them make the buying decision?
- Do they make decisions quickly?
- Do they need to compare your offer against offers from other companies?

Benefit Ideas

"People buy benefits."
  —Eric Lofholm

39. Tangible Benefits

Tangible benefits are benefits that produce definable results. Here are some examples:

- Make you more money
- Decrease employee turnover
- Live longer
- Save you money
- Save you time

40. Intangible Benefits

Intangible benefits are benefits that you can't measure. Here are some examples:

- Increased confidence
- Peace of mind
- Have more energy

41. Benefits of Taking Action

This is focusing the prospect on how they are going to benefit by purchasing your produce or service.

42. Consequences of Not Taking Action

This is focusing your prospect on the consequences of not taking action. This technique is used to sell life insurance. The salesperson focuses your attention on the consequences to you and your family if you don't have life insurance.

43. Benefit of the Benefit

The benefit of the benefit is how the prospect benefits from the main benefit of your product or service. Let's say you product helps your customers save $10,000 per month in expenses. The $10,000 savings is the main benefit. The question would be to the prospect how would you benefit from saving $10,000. In other words, what is the benefit to you, in what ways will saving $10,000 help you? They might say my wife could quit her job. Then you would say, "and what would that mean?"

When he tells you the benefit of his wife quitting her job he is sharing with you the benefit of the benefit. Always remember, "People buy benefits."

Rapport Techniques

44. Enter the World of Your Prospect and View Their Experience from Their Perspective

We each have our own model of the world. To gain a deeper level of rapport enter the world of the prospect and view their experience from their perspective.

45. Stay Present While You Are Delivering the Script

When you get really good at delivering your script it will be possible for you to deliver your script without staying present. Focus on being present with each prospect during every presentation.

Appointment Setting Techniques

46. Purpose of Setting Appointment Is to Set an Appointment

When you are creating your appointment setting script the focus is simply on setting the appointment. You are not trying to make a sale. Selling has a process to it. All you are trying to accomplish when setting an appointment is to set an appointment. This takes all of the pressure off.

47. Benefits of Setting the Appointment Are Different than the Benefits of the Appointment

There are the benefits of the appointment and then there are the benefits of your product or service. Here are some common benefits of an appointment:

- Free at your home
- At your office
- At a convenient time for you
- I will answer all of your questions

- I will share with you the benefits of how my product or service can help you.
- I will take the time to truly identify your needs; you will have the opportunity to move forward if you are comfortable. If not then no problem.

Appointment Setting Script Examples:

Voice Mail Script

Hi _____, this is _____ [say your name] from Eric Lofholm International. We are a sale straining firm. I am calling to speak with you about the president of our firm Eric Lofholm being a guest speaker at one of your upcoming sales meetings. Please call me back today at _____ [give your phone number].

Workshop Appointment Setting Script

Who would I speak with in regards to being a guest speaker at your office? Let them respond.

Can I speak with _____ [say name of person in charge of the meeting]?

Person answers.

Hi is _____ [say name of person in charge of the meeting] in? [Let them respond.]

Hi this is Kris Thompson. How are you today?

I represent national sales trainer Eric Lofholm. Eric asked me to give you a quick call today and offer you and your sales team a 30- to 60-minute customized sales training at your office on the topic of your choice.

The workshop is free.

The benefit to you is that your team will receive a motivational, professional sales training from the President of our firm Eric Lofholm. Eric normally charges $5,000 for a keynote speech, Eric recently moved to Northern California. For a limited time he is offering companies a free customized sales training on the topic of your choice for no charge. He is doing this to build up clientele in the area. Everyone in the meeting will get at least one great idea they can immediately implement.

Eric is only able to do a limited number of these workshops. I do have calendar openings now. What day do your normally have your meetings? [Let them respond.]

How many salespeople attend your meetings? [Let them respond.]

If they say they have five or more people, say:

How do you feel about scheduling a workshop? [Let them respond. If they agree to the workshop, say:]

Great, what is the address where the meeting will be held?

What time does the meeting start?

I am going to send you out an email confirmation. What is your email address?

Do you have other offices in the area?

If Eric were to be a guest speaker in all of your locations, who would be able to give us the green light to do so?

Objection Handling Techniques

Non-stated objection

Question

Solve the problem

Isolate

Bring out the objection

Script

Investigate

Before it comes up

Share the benefits

Reduce the risk

Be unreasonable

Negotiate

What would need to happen...

Objection Handling Scripts

Selling is like mental chess. Part of chess is anticipating your opponent's move. I do not view sales as a competition against the prospect but the concept is powerful.

There are typically 7 to 12 common objections in any industry. That is great news. You can choose to improve your objection handling techniques and responses.

The first step is to identify the common objections in your industry.

Use the list below to identify the common objections in your industry.

- I need to think about it.
- I don't have any money.
- I need to talk it over with someone.
- Can you fax me some information?
- I don't have the time.
- Your price is too high.
- I am already working with someone.
- We already tried it and it didn't work.
- I am not interested.

There are many ways to address these objections. Below are several different techniques.

48. Story

One of the most powerful ways to handle an objection is with a story. The reason why stories are so persuasive is they act as invisible selling. Stories also suspend time. Identify true stories that address the objection. One way to start off the story is by saying, "That reminds me of a story of a client who was in a similar situation. Let me share with you what they did."

One way to address an objection is with a story. Below is an example of this:

> The Prospect says the price is too high. You are offering a health product that costs $100 per month. Other than the price is their anything else preventing you from moving forward? [Isolate the objection; let them respond.]

Let me share with you a story I recently heard from a friend of mine named Eric. Eric's car battery needed to be replaced. He told his wife he would be dropping his car off at their local mechanics to have it done. He was going to get a ride from the mechanics to his office from one of his co-workers so she didn't need to worry about giving him a ride. She expected the battery would cost between $50 to $75.

About an hour after Eric dropped off the car his mechanic called him to let him know the regular services needed to be done on his car. The mechanic mentioned to Eric that since the car was already here he might as well get the servicing done. Eric agreed. About two hours later the mechanic called back to let Eric know while he was doing the servicing he noticed the brakes needed repair. Again, he suggested to Eric since the car is already here he might as well have the brakes done. Again, Eric agreed.

Around 4 o'clock Eric picked up the car. The total bill was around $350. On the way home Eric called his wife to let her know about the $350 charge on their debit card. Eric's wife handles the bank account so he wanted to let her know about the charge. When his wife heard the bill was $350 she was puzzled. She said to Eric I thought a battery was between $50 to $75. Eric then told her about the maintenance. She said $350, now that is expensive. Eric responded by saying actually it is extremely inexpensive. He told his wife the most inexpensive way to maintain a car is to do regular maintenance. The most expensive way to maintain a car is to fix it when it breaks down. Now that can cost thousands of dollars.

Your health is no different. The most inexpensive way to maintain your health is to do preventive maintenance. The most expensive way is to wait until something is wrong like needing to have your gallbladder taken out. If you really think about it your health is priceless would you agree? [Let them respond.]

My product is only $100 per month. You can expect to be healthier, have more energy and it is a preventative maintenance to help eliminate problems before they even come up. What do you say we give it a try? [Let them respond.]

49. Non-stated

Often times the true objection is a non-stated objection. The prospect states an objection, but it isn't the real one.

50. Question

You can answer an objection with a question. For example:

Objection: The price is too high.

Response: By too high what exactly do you mean?

Response: How much too much is it?

Response: Compared to what?

Objection: I don't have the time.

Response: When will you have the time?

Response: On a scale of 1 to 10, how motivated are you to move forward?

Response: What do you mean by that?

51. Solve the Problem

One way to handle an objection is to solve the problem.

If you were in the network marketing business you might invite a prospect to a hotel meeting on a Wednesday night. The prospect might say they can't get a babysitter. You could solve the problem by offering to have your sister baby sit.

52. Isolate

Isolating the objection is one of my favorite techniques. I like it because it is very effective and easy to learn. Here is an example:

Objection: I don't have the money.

Response: I can appreciate that. Other than the money is there anything else that is preventing you from taking action today? [Ask a closing question and be silent.]

Objection: I don't have the time.

Response: Other than the time, is there anything else preventing you from moving forward today?

53. Bring out the Objection

This is another very simple, yet very powerful technique. Bring out the objection is the opposite of isolate. Often times the true objection is a non-stated objection. Many times the prospect will not reveal the true objection. Each objection that they give you is a stall not an objection. When you use this technique it encourages the prospect to be honest with you. Here is an example:

Objection: I don't have the money.

Response: I understand. So what you are saying is that you don't have the money. Is that correct? [Repeated yes technique, ask a question and be silent.] Let them respond. I am sure that you have some other concerns before moving forward. Do you mind sharing those other concerns with me? [Let them respond.]

Objection: I need to think about it.

Response: I understand. Other than thinking about it I am sure that you have some other concerns. Do you mind sharing those other concerns with me?

54. Script Objection Responses

You can develop scripted responses to each objection. Here is an example:

Objection: I need to speak to my wife.

Response: I understand. So if your wife says yes, does that mean that you will do it? [Trial close.] Let them respond yes. Let me ask you a different question, what if she says no? [Trial close; ask a question for commitment and be silent.]

55. Investigate

Tell me more about that.

[After you say that phrase be silent.]

56. Before It Comes up

This is one of the most powerful objection handling techniques. You can reverse engineer your sales presentation to anticipate the objections that the prospect might bring up. You then can address the objections in the body of the sales presentation.

Here is an example of this technique: One of my clients sells $6,000 wealth building seminars. One of the objections is, "I am already a millionaire. What do I need your program for?" One of the scripts I created to handle this objection is:

> I am sure you are familiar with Donald Trump. Is that true? [Let them respond.]
>
> Would you agree that he is a great businessman? [Let them respond.]
>
> After Trump became a multi millionaire he made some bad financial decisions. In fact he lost so much money he went upside down $900 million. One day Trump was walking in downtown Manhattan with his then wife Marla Maples. He said, "Marla, you see that bum right there. He is worth $900 million more than I am."
>
> Although Trump is a great businessman he made some huge mistakes when it came to wealth building. If Trump was a client of ours we could have helped prevent him from losing his wealth.
>
> It is great that you have a net worth in the millions. We help clients like you not only increase your wealth but also preserve it. Some of our top clients are multimillionaires like yourself.

57. Share the Benefits

Objections are an opportunity to share the benefits. If the prospect says that insurance is not a good investment you can show them how it is a great investment.

58. Reduce the Risk

This means to change the offer. If you were asking for a six-month commitment, reduce the risk for the prospect by reducing the term to three months.

59. Be Unreasonable

This means to make an unreasonable request. For example ask the prospect to get second job so they can purchase your product or service. Suggest that they sell their car.

60. Negotiate

You can change the deal by negotiating. If I do this, will you do that?

If I lower the price by 5%, will you move forward today?

61. What Would Need to Happen?

Close the sale by asking a question.

- What would need to happen in order for you to move forward today?
- What would need to happen in order to get a check today?

Script Structure Techniques

62. Make List of Scripts You Need

Make a list of all of the scripts you would like to create.

Prioritize the list by importance.

Create an MS Word folder called "Scripts." Keep all of your work from this program in that folder.

Create a file for each script you want to create. Name the file, the name of the script you want to create. For example if you want to create a referral script, call the file "Referral Script."

Create a folder inside of the folder called "Scripts." Title the folder "Objections."

63. Make a List of the Common Objections in Your Industry.

Create a file inside the folder called "Objections" for each objection. Name the file after the name of the objections.

64. Front of the Room Syntax

I have sold millions of dollars of products and services using the front-of-the-room syntax below:

- Price
- What you get
- Bonus
- Drop sell

- Urgency
- Call to action

65. Sales Model

The sales model is the steps during the sales process. Identify the sales model for your product or service. Here are some examples of steps:

- Set appointment
- Mail information packet
- Confirmation call
- Run appointment and close
- Run appointment and set next appointment.

66. Reverse Engineer

This refers to your overall script. Begin with the end in mind. From that place, backtrack what needs to be in the script in order to move the prospect to action.

67. Objection Handling Structure

Make a list of all of the common objections in your industry. Create an MS Word Folder called "Objections." Inside the folder called Objections, create a Word document for each common objection. The name of the word document should be the name of the objection. Develop 10 to 20 responses for each of the common objections.

68. Benefits structure

Make a list of the benefits of your product or service. The list should include:

- Tangible benefits
- Intangible benefits
- Benefits of taking action
- Consequences of not taking action
- Benefit of the benefit

69. Appointment Setting Structure

The structure I used to write appointment-setting scripts is as follows:

- This is who I am.
- This is why I am calling.
- This is what I would like to do.
- Would you like to do it?

70. Ingredients of a Script

- Benefits
- Probing questions
- Offer
- Stories
- Objections

71. Syntax

The syntax is the order the script goes in. For example, identifying customer needs is going to go before the close.

72. Stage Selling/Benchmark Selling

Selling is a process. Stage selling or benchmark selling means you sell one step, stage, or benchmark at a time. You don't go to the next benchmark until the current benchmark is reached. The first step I teach is lead generation, then appointment setting, and then the sales presentation. In this example you don't deliver your sales presentation during the lead generation stage.

73. Conference Call Syntax

Below is the syntax to selling on a conference call. I have used this syntax to sell over $500,000 on conference calls.

- Intro
- Outcomes
- Chunk 1
- Chunk 2
- Call to action with a set time frame

Script Preparation Ideas

74. Prior to the Presentation Go over the Benefits/What You Want to Say/What Your Outcome Is/Any Objections They May Have

This tip is worth 100 times the investment in this book. Spend time preparing for each important sales call that you go on. You will not always have time to write down a word-for-word sales script and practice it. Prior to going on an important sales call review the benefits of your product or service, the likely objections you are going to get, your outcomes for the presentation, and the stories you are going to tell.

75. Practice Perfect

When practicing your script, practice perfect. In other words, practice the presentation word-for-word. Then, when you are on the live presentation, simply do the best you can.

76. Visualize a Successful Presentation

The subconscious mind does not know the difference between a real or imaginary event. By visualizing a successful sales call prior to the call, you are influencing the results that are going to happen during the call.

77. Define Your Outcomes for Your Presentation

Prior to going on your sales call define your outcomes for the presentation. Here are some examples of outcomes:

- Schedule the next appointment
- Generate 10 referrals
- Close the sale

Glasses Case History

When I went to buy some glasses, the script the store used was effective enough that I wrote it down later. It began when I said, "I am interested in getting some prescription sunglasses. Is that something you can help me with?"

"Do you have your prescription with you?"

"No."

"Would you like to schedule an eye exam to get a prescription?"

"Yes, how much is it?"

"$54. Would you like having an exam right now?"

"Yes."

"Come over here and have a seat. I have some paperwork for you to fill out."

I filled out the paperwork.

"Do you have insurance?"

"I do but I don't know if I have a vision plan."

"Do you have a AAA card?"

"Yes."

"We can offer you a 30% discount if your insurance plan doesn't cover vision."

The exam started.

"Did they explain to you how the pricing works?"

"Yes, they told me it would be $54."

"That is correct. For our basic exam the price is $54. We also offer a comprehensive exam for $93. (He points to a machine that has a picture of a giant red eye behind it. The picture implies that the machine will give the doctor some type of advanced look at your eye that changes the color of your eye in some way."

I figured, why not, for an extra $39 I can get the fancy exam, whatever that is.

"Would you like the comprehensive exam?"

"Yes."

He did the exam.

"The doctor will see you now."

"You are here to get a new prescription for your glasses?"

"What brought me in was I want to get some sunglasses that are prescription. They told me I needed to get an eye exam. I might also be interested in some contacts as well."

"Let's take a look." She further examined my eyes.

"I am going to recommend pupil dilation. It takes about 20 minutes. Once your pupils are dilated I will exam them again. Would you like me to do the pupil dilation?"

"Sure."

"While you are waiting, why don't you go and look at some glasses?"

The doctor handed me off to another woman. This was the fourth person I had been in contact with. The script was working perfectly. Each person knew their job. I was now with the closer. She informed me that my prescription had slightly changed and now I would need a new pair of glasses as well as the sunglasses.

"Let's take a look at some frames."

She led me to the regular frames and the sunglasses frames. We picked out several pairs. She complimented me on how good I looked in glasses. She told me that I could wear almost any pair and I'd look great. I was feeling great now.

We sat down and I started to ask her about prices. My budget in my mind was $200. If it cost more than $200 I was going to walk.

She let me know that I could have a six-months same-as-cash plan on approval with zero down. I could even finance the $93 eye exam. She asked me if I would like to apply. I told her yes.

She gathered the information to run my credit. She got approval 8 seconds later. She told me my credit was so good I got instant approval. Again, I felt great.

I started to think, "Forget about $200, I have 6 months same as cash. That is practically free."

I was now in the shopping mood. I asked her how much the sports goggles were.

She told me $119. I grabbed a pair off the shelf and put them on the desk.

She let me know my current frames would work or I could get a brand new frame for only$53. She added it all up. The total was $727.63. She was silent.

I decided, "Okay, I'll take it." I walked into the store to inquire about getting some prescription glasses. I walked out of the store the proud owner of a new pair of sunglasses, a new pair of glasses, and a pair of sports goggles. I still needed to get my contacts. That would probably be another $100.

This was not a word-for-word script. It was several scripts inside of one big script. What makes it work was the syntax or order the script went in.

Bonus Chapter #2

10 Sample Probing Questions Scripts

Here are ten scripts for probing questions and statements. Borrow these, or use them as templates for designing your own.

1. What type of budget do you have to work with?
2. How soon would you like to get started?
3. Have you ever worked with a realtor before?
4. Where do you currently buy your office supplies?
5. Have you ever been professionally trained in sales?
6. How would you rate your sales skills on a scale of 1 to 10?
7. What result would make the biggest impact on your business right now?
8. Tell me about your situation.
9. Describe to me your dream job.
10. Describe your credit to me.

10 Sample Closing Scripts

1. If I can reduce your monthly payments and get you $10,000 in cash at close would you like to refinance your mortgage?

2. How do you feel about getting started today?

3. Based on our discussion, how do you feel about moving forward?

4. Which credit card would you like to use today?

5. We can do a three-month or four-month listing. What would work best for you?

6. Put your name here.

7. Learn more on a webinar tomorrow, May 15 at 9:15am Pacific. To join the webinar go to **http://saleschampion.com/go/coach/**.

8. It would really help me out if you could buy some cookies from my daughter for the Girl Scouts. Most people are buying five boxes. Could you buy at least two?

9. Would you like to take advantage of the 50% discount we're running this week?

10. If you'd like to take advantage of this opportunity to save 25% on your remaining payment installments, email me at **eric@lofholm.com**.

Bonus Chapter #4

Sample Referral Script

Nielsen research shows that 92 percent of people trust referrals more than any other form of marketing. A good referral system is one of the most effective lead generation systems you can have. Here is a sample referral script you can adapt for your own use.

A Sample Referral Script

As you probably know, I work with referrals. A good referral for me is a sales manager or network marketing leader who has a team of six or more people here in Southern California.

Industries I work in, in addition to yours are real estate, mortgage, network marketing, insurance, and auto sales.

When you think of a good referral think of other offices your company has, where you have worked in the past, where you client work, and people who have sold to you.

Of everyone you know who would be the best referral for me?

Why do you say that?

Does anyone else come to mind?

Why do you say that?

Does anyone else come to mind?

Why do you say that?

Does anyone else come to mind?

Why do you say that?

Does anyone else come to mind?

10 Sample Email Subject Line Scripts

1. Would you like a powerful sales script for your sales team?

2. I need your help

3. This is what you are missing out on...

4. I want to coach you today at 4:00 PM pacific and share 7 of my BEST ideas with you

5. 2 Great Free Sales Trainings—Closing (Fri) Scripting (Tues)

6. Proteges, 6 Months of Sales Training in ONE day!

7. Script Writing Webinar is today at 4:00 PM Pacific

8. Wanted: Sales Superstar Candidates

9. I am looking for 12 people who want to sprint with me!

10. 7 slots have been filled. I have 5 slots left for those who want to blitz with me!

Bonus Chapter #6

Sample
Conference Call Script

In this chapter I'm going to include a transcript of a conference call that I did where I sold a boot camp during a conference call. You can hold conference calls to:

- Generate Leads
- Set Appointments
- Make Sales

Outline

The outline to use is:

    I. Intro

   II. Outcomes

  III. Chunk 1

  IV. Chunk 2

   V. Chunk 3

  VI. Call to Action

Intro: This section lasts 2 to 7 minutes. During this section you are introducing you, your company, and your credibility. This is a great place to tell your story.

Outcomes: In this section state the outcomes for the call. I usually have two outcomes for the call. The first outcome is to add value by providing the promised call content. My second outcome is to offer my program or offer a consultation.

Chunk: A chunk is a section of content. One of my chunks is a section where the prospect imagines how their life would be different. For example: Imagine your sales scripts are done and the money is rolling in how would you life be different? A great technique is to embed success stories in your chunks.

Call to Action: In this section you offer your product, service, consultation, or appointment.

Transcript

Title: How to Grow Your Business Using Sales Scripts Conference Call

Intro

Hi this is Eric Lofholm and I would like to welcome all of you to the very special conference call. We're going to be talking about my very favorite subject on selling which is How to Grow Your Business Using Sales Scripts.

The reason why this topic is the most favorite of all the different topics that I could train on, this is the topic that has made me the most money. It is the topic that increased sales for me the most. Also, it's very fun for me to teach this topic because it is misunderstood by so many people. After listening to me tonight, the light bulb is going to go off for so many of you and I'm going to open up a whole new way of thinking about sales scripts.

I want to start off and acknowledge you for being on this call and being open-minded enough to the idea that sales scripting is something that could help you increase your results.

The reality is most sales people resist scripting. The reason they resist scripting is they have a negative view on scripting. In fact, they're not really sure even what scripting is and yet they resist it. You guys are open to the idea that your results could grow using scripts. So I acknowledge you for being on the call.

But here's how the call's going to go. I've got two outcomes for my presentation.

Outcomes

My first outcome is to share with you some great specific ideas on how to use sales scripting to increase your results.

I am an expert at sales scripting. I've been using scripts now for the last fifteen years and teaching people how to use scripts in their business for the last ten. So, I'm going to give you some great, great content tonight.

My second outcome is the world's greatest sales mind who also happens to be my mentor, Dr. Donald Moine. He and I are going to be teaching a two-day, we call it our self-presentation boot camp. I use the word "presentation"—it means the same as a sales script. So it's a scripting presentation boot camp February 23rd and 24th. It's the only one that we're scheduled to teach together this year. It's in Los Angeles and at the very end of the call, after I've delivered tremendous content to you, I'm going to extend a very special invitation to you.

I've put something together extra-special for all of you that are listening in on tonight's call and I'm going to give you the details on that at the very end of the call.

My Story

My start in sales. I drifted into sales like so many of us. I don't know. Did any of you on this call, when you were in high school, dream some day you'd be in commissioned sales and have the stress and pressure of having an up-and-down results in selling like we all, most of us anyway, experience?

I ended up working for a real estate investor and he offered me; that was part time as his assistant and the other part-time I did inside sales.

I started off doing telemarketing and I was terrible at it. At the end of my first year, I'd missed quota two months in a row and a manager, Richard Hogan, pulled me into the office and said, "Eric, selling's not for everybody and it's probably not for you. If you don't hit your quota this next month then we're going to let you go."

My back was against the wall and I had to somehow some way hit quota, then I didn't know how to sell. I was right on the verge of being fired.

This is when I met Dr. Donald Moine. He's the author of *Unlimited Selling Power*, of which *Success Magazine*, when it existed, said "*Unlimited Selling Power* is one of the ten best books ever written on the subject of professional selling."

Dr. Moine, through a series of events that came into my life, began to mentor and coach me. It was kind of like Obi-Wan Kenobi when he met Luke Skywalker in the Star Wars movie that came out in the mid-seventies.

So, he took me under his wing and he began to mentor and coach me. When you're getting coached by somebody at that level, you would expect my results to go up. They did. Initially they barely went up.

The quota was ten thousand in gross sales. With Dr. Moine's help I did ten thousand five hundred in gross sales. I made it by a single month and, more importantly, I was able to keep my job.

Well the next month I did $51,000 in gross sales and seven months later I did $160,000 in gross sales. In less than a year, I went from almost being fired to $160,000 in gross sales in a few single months. Want to know how I did it? Sales scripting.

Dr. Moine taught me how to harness the power of sales scripting. I went from almost being fired to the top producer in the company in less than a year by understanding sales scripting. I wasn't making more calls. I wasn't believing that higher level. I had the right words to make the sale.

You can be motivated; you could have a great company to represent; you can have great products and services but at the end of the day, you have to have the right words. So, that's what this conversation is about.

How do you improve the quality of your words?

Now, I want you to imagine that you have this awesome sales script on your products and services. Maybe you have three scripts and you've got three main products; or one main product—however many products you offer, you've got these awesome, killer sales scripts.

Think about what would happen to you in your results. It's very possible that you would go to number one company; you would be winning the trips; you'd be taking the recognition; you're income would explode; you would be a hero with your family. All these opportunities would open up for you. And that's what has happened for me over these last fifteen years, once I learned the power of sales scripting.

Part of Selling Is Education. I am Educating the Prospect Here

Before we embrace sales scripting, we have to embrace the idea of selling. So many people resist sales and the reason why they resist selling is: We were all in a seminar together right now and I said, "When you think of a salesperson, what do you think of?"

The number one thing that people say is negative: arm-twisting, high-pressure, manipulation, in it for themselves.... Used car sales is the most common example that people use with an industry. It's what people think of sales. It tends to be negative.

There's a problem with that because if you embrace being a salesperson—I'm going to take it even a step further—if you're not proud to be a salesperson, what you're doing is you're putting an imaginary hurdle in front of you that's going to prevent you from achieving your potential.

We don't have a lot of time to focus on changing your mindset, but I'm just going to give you a couple of quick ideas.

It's important that you learn how to embrace sales because that's the prerequisite in order to harness the power of sales scripting.

To me, the definition of "selling" is that "selling equals service." When you sell, sell from honesty, integrity and compassion. It's not about hard-sell, it's about heart-sell.

Selling is about leading and it is about moving people to action. I want you to be open to the idea of being proud of being a salesperson. And for so many of you, you know our culture says selling is negative, but that doesn't mean selling is negative.

There was a time when they said the world was flat, but that didn't mean that the world was flat. See?

"The world is flat" is very similar to saying "selling is negative." Selling is not negative. Selling is a wonderful, wonderful thing. It's just misunderstood by a lot of people. I'm proud to be in sales and I'm proud to teach others to be proud of being in sales. Because, for you, it could be life-changing.

ICR

Tonight's call could be the most important call you've ever been on in your entire life! This is the number one skill-set that I've developed through the years that has made the biggest difference in my sales results.

So, now, let's say you're open to the idea of embracing sales; or even you're willing to take the step of starting to affirm that you're proud of being in sales.

Education

The next step is to embrace sales scripting. For those of you on the call that have had a resistance to scripting yet you still came to the call today, I acknowledge you because I'm going to give you a whole new way of looking at what sales scripting is.

Mindreading

Most people, when they think of a script, they think it's "canned, rehearsed, mechanical, inauthentic, it's just not me," and that's not what a script is.

The definition of a script is words in sequence that have meaning. So, if you're saying words and you're making sense, you're using a script. You're either using a script or your speaking in gibberish and none of you on this call speak in gibberish.

It's not a question of whether or not you're using a script, the question is how effective are your scripts. You see, if you're winging it, which is how most people operate; and it's not a bad thing, it's just what's so. Most people are not placed where they resisted scripting, then what are you left with. If you resist this type of scripting I'm going to train you on, then you're left with winging it. So I want you to get something very powerful.

Winging it is a script. When you wing it, after four or five times, you start developing patterns with your "winging-it" scripts. You start saying the same things over and over and over again and when you wing it, you get wing-it results.

This is not what the professionals do. Certainly not what I do. It is not what I train my superstar clients to do. As many of the people that I work with, they started off just average, okay sales people. They weren't sales superstars and they learned how become sales superstars with my help. I taught them these powerful distinctions and it's made all the difference in the world for them. They can make all the difference in the world for you as well.

Convincer

I want to read to you from Michael Gerber's book, *The E Myth*, and many of you are familiar with that book. Michael Gerber is regarded by many as one of the top experts in the world on business and how to grow businesses.

In his book, I'm quoting his book word-for-word here:

> Sales systems. Things need to be sold and it's usually people who have to sell them. Everyone in business has heard the old song, 'eighty percent of our sales are produced by twenty percent of our people. Unfortunately, few seem to know what the twenty percent are doing that the eighty percent aren't.

> Well, let me tell you, the twenty percent are using a system and the eighty percent are not. A selling system is a...system and I've seen such systems produce one hundred percent to five hundred percent increase in sales in almost no time.

> What is a selling system? It's a voice-orchestrated interaction between you and your customer that follows five primary steps.

> Step number one: Identification of the specific benchmark or consumer decision points in your selling process.

And listen to what Gerber says:

> The mere scripting of the words that will get you to each one successfully [yes] written down like the script for a play.

> The creation of various material to be used with each script. The memorization of each benchmark's script. The delivery of each script by your salesperson in identical fashion.

> The career development company we worked with put it in the hands of people with no experience and revenue was increased by three hundred percent. These weren't sales people! They had no experience and company results went up three hundred percent.

> An advertising agency put it in the hands of people with no experience in either selling or advertising and revenue was increased five hundred percent in two years.

> A health spa put it in the hands of people with no experience and revenue was increased forty percent in two months.

So, take it from Michael Gerber, one of the top experts in the world, sales scripting absolutely works.

Now, the next distinction that I want to share with you is—some of you on this call, you have a team of people. You're either a business owner and you've got people that work for you as sales, you're a VP of sales or a sales manager if you a team of people beneath you, or you're in network marketing and you have an organization.

So, this is a distinction around using scripts and then sharing them with your entire team. I'm going to share this distinction with you with a story.

One of the most powerful sales scripts that you can use are success stories. So, if you're taking notes, you can jot this down, "Nothing sells like success."

Nothing sells like success.

Success Story

There's a very successful businesswoman named Loral Langemeier. Some of you know who Loral is, her website is live out loud dot com. She has best-selling books and a multi-million-dollar company.

Many years ago, Loral came to me and she realized that she needed scripts for her inside sales team. Loral hired me. She paid me a fee of five thousand dollars and she put me on her team and I started writing scripts for her.

What I explained to Loral is, I said, "You're going to make this initial investment. Then I'm going to get some scripts done for you. We're going to get them in the hands of your team and we're going to train them. Your team is then going to increase their results and then we're going to take a small percentage of your profit and then you're going to reinvest with me and I'm going to continue to work with you and your team."

Everything I said just now is what I told Loral and it is exactly what happened. I did consulting for her team for eighteen months. So, she came out-of-pocket, one-time with a five thousand dollar investment and then took a small portion and reinvested in the profit.

I helped take her inside sales team from fifty thousand a month to over a million a month in gross sales. That's a small example, a powerful example, of harnessing the power of sales scripts.

Benefit

You see, once a script is created, you have the benefit of that script for the rest of your career. Loral's team is still benefitting from some of the scripts that I wrote several years ago.

The most powerful human force on the planet is the power of suggestion! So, I want to make a suggestion for all of you that have a team. If you want to get scripts done for your team and then share them with your entire organization and you can positively increase the results across the board of your company.

The next thing I want to talk about are different types of scripts. We have: appointment-setting scripts; telephone scripts, if you give your sales presentation over the phone; face-to-face scripts, if you meet with your prospects. There are referral scripts, objection-handling scripts, things to say when a prospect says, "I don't have the money. I don't have the time. I need to think about it."

The number one reason I have found why salespeople are not effective with handling objections is they haven't taken the time to develop powerful scripts. Then to internalize those scripts. Then when in a real live sales situation they are able to confidently come back and move the prospect to action.

Then there's front-of-the-room scripts, if you do front-of-the-room selling.

I have a lot of public speakers that come to me and seek out my help. The reason why is because they are doing front-of-the-room presentations but they're not closing.

You want to know why they're not closing? They don't have the right scripts. Because then when I help them get the right script, in some cases they go from making five hundred to a thousand dollars a speech, to over ten thousand dollars a speech!

Success Story

I had a client come to me recently and she was really uncomfortable with her script. So I helped her with the script. No exaggeration, the first time she went to use it, you're not going to believe what I'm going tell you, but it's true, she generated a hundred thousand dollars in sales in ninety minutes. She was on a 50–50 with the promoter.

She pocketed $50,000 off of one presentation because she had the right script. Without the right script, she might have sold nothing.

Then there are conference-call scripts, if any of you do selling in conference calls.

Now the interesting thing about referral scripts is, I have people come to me all the time that say, "Eric, I ask for referrals and I just never get any." And, what I share with them is you've figured out scripts on how to not get referrals.

I want to give you a very powerful idea now. I'd like you to jot it in your notes. It goes like this: Human beings respond in predictable ways. Human beings respond in predictable ways.

If you ask for referrals and you consistently don't get them, then you've figured out a script on how to not get referrals.

If you're asking for the order and you keep getting, "Your price is too high. Your price is too high. Your price is too high," you've figured out a script that causes the response "Your price is too high." Virtually every sales challenge, as far as the presentation is concerned, can be solved using sales scripting.

In sales, we are wordsmiths. Jot this phrase in your notes, "My words will make me rich." It's the words that you use.

You've probably all heard the expression, "It takes money to make money." Well, that's not true in sales.

Humor

In sales we use words to create money out of thin air. In sales, we go, "Blah, blah, blah, blah, blah, blah, blah, blah, blah."—Poof! $500. "Blah, blah, blah, blah, blah, blah, blah, blah, blah."—Poof! $5,000.

My most successful sales day ever, "Blah, blah, blah, blah, blah, blah, blah, blah, blah."—Poof! $70,000. Not a bad day!

That was made possible because of sales scripting. Without sales scripting, that $70,000 day probably would have been a $700 day.

Sales scripting is so important. It should be. You know, to become a doctor, you have to go to college and you have to go to medical school and take very strenuous tests. It takes many, many years in order for you to become a doctor. You probably invest $100,000 to $200,000 in order to become a doctor.

It should be required, it's not, but it should be, to become a professional sales person; that you go to college and get a degree in selling and invest $50,000 to

$100,000 and one of the required courses will be how to write a sales script. If that was true, if you had to invest $50,000 to $100,000 and learn how to write a sales script, it would pay for itself double, triple, five times, ten times over, just like a doctor.

Because in sales, we all have the opportunity to earn $100,000 a year, $200,000 a year, $500,000 a year! My goal this year—I can't even believe that it's this, but it is—my goal is to net, after expenses, $1 million this year. Without sales scripting, I would be, like, shooting for $50,000.

Now let's talk about the components of a sales script because, when you start writing your script, you don't just sit down and say, "Well, what's the first thing I say? What's the second thing?" You don't just do that. That's not the way to write a sales script.

Building Value in the Participant Being on the Call

What I'm going to share with you right now has taken me ten years to figure out what I'm about to teach you.

In working with Dr. Moine, I invested over $30,000, hiring Dr. Moine to work with him in seminars and work with him one-on-one to learn this information. Am I glad I did it? Absolutely! It generated over $3 million in income from a direct result of what I've learned from Dr. Moine. So I'm very glad I made that investment.

ICR

What I'm about to tell you has taken me years to learn and it's going to cut your learning curve down so much and I'm so glad that you're on the call right now to share what I'm about to tell you.

It's the components of the sales scripts. You see, when you write a script, it's kind of like baking a cake. When you bake a cake, you go look in your pantry and say, 'well, Do I have the cake mix?' and 'Do I have the flour?' and blah, blah—the butter and do I have the egg—Do I have all the ingredients that I need?

So you might look in the pantry and maybe you're missing some of the ingredients in your refrigerator. So you go down to the grocery store before you start cooking the cake and make sure you have all the ingredients.

Then, once you have the ingredients, then you're going to bake the cake. So, that's very similar as writing a sales script.

By the way, the technique I just used in scripting is called connect the known to the unknown. Connect the known to the unknown.

I gave you something that you can relate with which is baking a cake and I connected something that's new to you, for most of you, writing your own sales scripts.

At the sales presentation boot camp that I'm going to invite you to at the end of this call, I'm going to teach you over seventy different scripting techniques. The exact formula that I use to write my own scripts.

If I was to write a script for you right now; if I was coaching you to write a script, I would start with what I'm going to tell you to do right now.

You want to get the ingredients of the script and here are the ingredients and you definitely want to write this down.

The first ingredient is stories and the next ingredient is probing questions and the next ingredient is the offer. It goes: stories, probing questions, offer.

Then the next ingredient is objections and then the last ingredient is benefits.

What I would do—not only am I telling you exactly what to do to get your scripts started, I'm going to give you a very important tip. It may not sound like a lot, but it's really, really valuable, what I'm about to tell you. If I didn't tell you this, you'd start doing this on scraps of paper and your work would be all over the place.

What I want you to do, most of you use Microsoft Word, now I want you to create a folder in Microsoft Word called "Scripts" and then I want you to create word documents inside that folder called "Stories" and then call another Word document "Probing Questions" then call another Word document "Offer" and then another Word document "Objections" and then another Word document "Benefits."

You're going to label your stories "nothing sells like success." I shared a success story with you a moment ago about Loral Langemeier. I'm going to share another success story with you right now to help motivate and inspire you to get your scripts done.

This is a story about one of my star clients named Arvee Robinson. Arvee coaches people on how to front-of-the-room speaking to grow their businesses. And when I met Arvee, she's fantastic at what she does. Her website is instant pro speaker dot com.

So she didn't need any help getting better at coaching people, but she wasn't attracting enough clients. Some of you, maybe you can relate with this where, maybe you're a real estate agent and you feel that you're a lot better agent than somebody else in your office but they're getting more deals than you.

And you think, "But I'm better than them."

Or maybe you're a financial advisor and you're like, "I'm a much better financial advisor than Paul, but Paul's doubling my income. What's wrong here?"

And this is what happens with so many people. They're really, really good at what they do but they haven't yet developed a skill set to articulate to somebody else about what they do. They move them to action.

That's the challenge that some of you are having right now. If you're really passionate and you believe in what you do, but you're not communicating it to somebody else in a way—you're not using scripts in a way that makes it compelling to move them to action. So that was Arvee's challenge.

Then, when I met her she was making about four thousand dollars a month. She resisted sales scripting. She was not…She resisted being a salesperson. She thought sales was arm-twisting, high-pressure and manipulative.

Success Story

So I helped Arvee overcome that. Then I helped Arvee embrace sales scripting and I taught her my script-writing formulas.

One of the things that Arvee wanted to do was raise her price points. Some of you that are coaches and consultants or if you could adjust your pricing structure, you can use scripts to raise your price points. She doubles her coaching fee and she got a full practice coaching because she can prove the quality of her sales script which increased her confidence.

Last year, Arvee bumped her income from $4,000 a month—she's now making $15,000 to $20,000 a month.

Last year she had been renting for the last eight years and she went and bought a home. She became a homeowner again for the first time in eight years.

That's one of the benefits of scripting is you have to figure out what to do with all the extra money that you're making.

So, Arvee is making all this extra money and she's like, "I need a tax write-off and I want to get my dream home." So she went and bought this dream resort home with a beautiful pool in the back yard.

So that was an example of a success story. I call that "The Arvee Robinson Story."

Or the story I shared with you earlier is "The Loral Langemeier Story."

In my Microsoft Word document- inside of my folder called "Scripts," I'd write "The Loral Langemeier Story" and "The Arvee Robinson Story"—and you'll want to do that as well.

Then "Probing Questions." The easiest way to persuade or influence somebody is to find out what they want and give it to them. The way you find out what they want is by asking questions.

You want to make a laundry list of the questions that you ask your prospects. You don't want to wing-it when it comes to the questions. You want to know what questions you're going to ask in advance. So create that laundry list of probing questions.

The next one is the offer. This refers to the close.

What I want here is a laundry list of all the component of the close. The price. Guarantee, if you have one. The bonuses or incentives for taking action. The warranty. The contract. The payment terms; how you accept payment.

Whether you accept cash, check, credit cards, Visa, American Express, MasterCard or you'll invoice them. What's included in the offer. Everything they're going to receive and then a call to action.

People need to be led and you need to be clear with people. One of the things that critical in the close that it's clear and compelling. If we create a clear and compelling close, you've got to figure out what are the ingredients of the close. That's your laundry list. A laundry list for the offer.

The next one is the objections. You need a laundry list of all of the objections. I don't have the money. I don't have the time. I need to think about it. Can you send me some information.

We need to know all those objections, then we need to figure out how we're going to address those objections when they come up. Are we going to address them in the script in the body of the presentation or are we going to address them after they come up?

You must develop, you must develop, powerful, persuasive scripts when it comes to objection handling. All sales people, the person says, "I need to think about it." And the salesperson goes, "Okay. How long do you need to think about it?" They say, "Well, till tomorrow." Okay, "I'll call you tomorrow." Wrong!

You need to add a powerful script. Be able to address that objection and move the prospect to action. If you're not converting when you're getting objections—and that doesn't mean you close every sale—but if you're getting objections, I want you to ask yourself this question and be honest with yourself: Are you effective at moving people to action when you get objections?

If the answer is "no" you're leaving thousands of dollars on the table. It's really, really important that you develop the skill-set to get effective at objection handling.

Then the last laundry list is the laundry list of benefits. I'm going to give you five different aspects of benefits. At the end of the day, people buy benefits.

You might have heard this expression that people buy you. Not true. Yes, you need to feel trust and rapport and absolutely you want to be likeable. People are not going to part with their hard-earned cash just because they like you. They're going to part with their hard-earned cash because you've clearly communicated that your product or service delivers benefits that they want.

You have to know what are the benefits of your product and service and then you've got to figure out how to communicate those benefits in the body of the presentation.

Now I'm going to give you five different aspects of benefits.

The first aspect is a tangible benefit. A tangible benefit is something that makes you money, it saves you time, it decreases employee turnover. These are all tangible benefits.

Then we've got intangible benefits. Things like peace of mind, increased confidence. You can't quite put your finger on it, but people want those benefits. More energy. Those are intangible benefits.

Then you've got the benefits of taking action. These are the benefits for taking action now.

Success Story

Then you've got the consequences of not taking action. This is how life insurance is sold. Somebody sold, my life insurance salesperson, his name is Doug Bell and he's a wonderful, wonderful salesperson. What got me to take action is Doug said, "Eric, let me ask you a question. You're the main bread winner in your family and, heaven something should happen to you and you passed away, would your wife be able to make the mortgage payment in your current home?"

I said, "I never really thought about it."

He said, "Well, think about it. Would she be able to make the mortgage payments?"

"Well, I guess not."

Then Doug said, "Well, heaven forbid if something happened to you, would you like your children and your wife to still be able to live in their home?"

I said, "Well, of course."

So, he got me associated to the consequences of not having life insurance because my family would have to move.

I have peace of mind knowing right now—We have no crystal ball in when our last day is—and I have peace of mind knowing that my family would be financially taken care of. My children would live a nice life and my wife would be able to live a nice comfortable life.

That was one of the things that he did in his script that moved me to action. There's many others. Doug, by the way, is a client of mine. I taught him many of these scripts that he used to win me, to move me to action on a very large life insurance policy, which I'm happy to own.

So, that's the consequences of not taking action and the last benefit is the real reason why people buy and this is called the benefit of the benefit.

The benefit of the benefit is when somebody does business with you, what do they get out of it after they enjoy your product or service.

For example, with sales scripting. The benefit of sales scripting is that you have a script done that will help you make more sales.

Then what's the benefit of that? Well, you make more money.

What's the benefit of that? Then you can pay off all your credit card debt.

Do you realize right now that you could pay off your credit debt one hundred percent by having effective sales scripts? That's the benefit of the benefit.

Or you might want to buy your own home, like Arvee did. Arvee was able to buy her own home. That was the benefit of the benefit of sales scripting. You want to get connected to what's the benefit of the benefit of your product or service.

The next thing I want to talk about are script writing techniques.

One technique is to create a baseline script by writing down what you currently say. The way you do that is you take a tape recorder with you and you record your presentation. Then you transcribe it. That will give you your baseline script.

The next technique is you could borrow somebody else's scripts. Human beings respond in predictable ways. So what that means is, you listen to someone else's presentation and you like what they say? You can then borrow what they say. You can model what they say and incorporate that into your presentation. That, by the way, is a million-dollar idea.

The next idea is to tell yourself that you're a script writer. I want you to embrace sales scripting. Don't resist it. Embrace it. Embrace the skill set that, you know, in all honesty, could be the most important skill set that you ever develop in business.

Once they help Loral out, she'll make millions of dollars every year for the rest of her business career because she's now harnessed the power of sales scripting.

My vision for Arvee Robinson is that she goes to $100,000 a month in gross revenue.

I've lived it myself! I've gone from being a terrible sales person to now earning an income I never would have dreamed of years ago. I'm living the life the of my dreams! I live in my dream home. I drive my dream car. I live my life on my terms. I get to go on wonderful vacations.

And I don't say that to brag. I say that to demonstrate that what's caused these incredible results for me is understanding sales scripting. All I had to do to learn it, the way I do it, is I invested thirty thousand dollars with Dr. Moine and I made a decision that I was going to stay in the conversation with Dr. Moine on an ongoing basis to develop these sales scripting tools.

It was the greatest business decision that I ever made in my life. At the end of my call tonight, I have an opportunity for every single one of you on this call to learn my script-writing formulas and to enter into a conversation with me, just like I have with Dr. Moine, I'm going to offer you a life-time opportunity to work with me.

I'm so excited about offering this! Some of you on this call, you're already motivated. You've got a great product or service to sell. The only thing that you're missing is having the right words.

You're going to have to be trained just like a doctor gets trained, just like I got trained. I didn't roll out of bed one day and miraculously know how to write sales scripts. I went and got trained by the greatest sales mind in the world.

When I extend this invitation at the end of the call, not only am I going to train you, Dr. Moine's going to train you as well. This will be the most powerful boot camp you've ever attended in your life. You're going to harness the power of sales scripting just like Arvee Robinson and Loral Langemeier and some of my other star clients.

It will be life-changing for you. If you have credit card debt, you'll be able to pay it off once and for all. If you want to become a homeowner; if you want to become number one in your company…

Success Story

I helped Joey Aszterbaum, his website is **joeyloans.com**, I trained Joey with my script writing formulas. He's been number one the last two years at his company.

Last year his goal was to do 48 loans. With my help, he did 67 loans in a down market. He's in Hawaii right now with his wife on an all-expenses-paid trip because he harnessed the power of sales scripting. His results went up when most loan officers—some of their results went down and some of them completely got out of the business. That's the power of sales scripting.

Let's talk back into the content. I have some more powerful ideas to share with you right now.

The next idea is to tell success stories, which I touched on earlier; then the next idea is to reverse-engineer your script.

What this means is, you think about at the end of your presentation, what's the result that you want to have happen from your script. Then, reverse-engineer what you have to say during your script in order to produce that result.

So, on Saturday I taught a seminar and my goal was to get 2,000 referrals? Can you believe that? I had a goal to get 2,000 referrals; so that was my goal.

So I reverse-engineered it and I used a script and some of you on the call right now, you were there; I got 1,725 referrals out of a group of about 150 people because of harnessing the power of sales scripting.

The distinction I'm teaching is called "Reverse-Engineer." First I had to figure out what I wanted then I had to figure out what I need to say in order to get what I wanted.

Can you believe that? I got 1,725 referrals from a live audience! Incredible harnessing the power of sales scripting!

The next thing I want to share with you—this is so important—you need to know what your sales model is. You need to know what your sales model is. A sales model is like a one-call close or set appointment; one-call, two-call close.

The Girl Scouts, they do a one-call close. Their script is, "Would you like to buy some Girl Scout Cookies?"

That's the whole script. That script sells 5 million boxes of Girl Scout Cookies a year! Can you believe that? The script is—one of the Girl Scouts has the script. Not the mom. It doesn't work when the mom says it. So, that's a one-call close.

Then you've got set appointment/one-call close. That's like a real estate agent doing a listing presentation. They set the appointment and they go meet with the husband, wife or person selling the property. Then they ask for the listing at the end of the first appointment.

It doesn't mean that's when they get the listing. It means that's when they close. It's when they ask for the listing.

A financial advisor usually do set appointment, one-call, two-call close. They set an appointment then they go on the appointment then they go on another appointment then they ask for the order. You have to ask for the order at the end of your presentation.

I know that some of you on this call are giving presentations and you're not asked for the order. Or you're getting to the end of the presentation and you're not asking for the order powerfully. You're lacking confidence in the close and the reason why people lack confidence in the close? Nine out of ten times it's because they don't have an effective script.

When they get to the close and they lack confidence. If that's you right now, you're leaving thousands of dollars on the table.

You deserve to be confident in the close. You owe it to yourself to get the proper training. Have an effective script. Be powerful. Be confident in the close.

What we're going to do next is an, "Oh, let-me-finish-up sales model."

So, you've got to figure out what your sales model is, right? Just make a note to yourself, "I need to know what my sales model is."

Then the next thing you need is your script outline. Your script outline. A typical script outline is introduction, trust and rapport, identify customer needs, bring the benefits to light by telling success stories, do the close, handle objections then after doing the close you follow up. That's a very generic script outline. You need to know what your outline is.

First you figure out your sales model, then you figure your outline, then you've got the ingredients of your scripts (stories, probing questions, offer, objections and benefits) and then from there you create your scripts.

The next thing that we're going to do is an exercise. I want you to make a laundry list right now, the scripts that you need. As you're writing these down I'll prompt you with some ideas. It's really important for you to do this exercise right now.

- If you need an appointment-setting script, write that down. If you need the referral-script, write that down.
- Every or product or service that you offer—you need a script for that. You need a script for every product or service.
- If you do front-of-the-room selling, you need a script for that.
- If you do telephone sales, you need a script for that.
- You also need objection-scripts.
- If you're in network marketing, you need recruiting-scripts.
- If you hire people for your company, you need hiring-scripts.
- You also need follow-up-scripts.

Right. Now, you've got your list of scripts. I want you to imagine that those scripts are now done. You've got powerful, persuasive scripts. You're more confident in the close. The scripts are moving people to action.

How much more money would you make in 2008 if you had those scripts right now? Could you make an extra $10,000? $20,000? $50,000 or more?

Now, I want you to imagine how much longer do you plan on being in business. You may have never thought of this before. I'm 37. I plan on being in business until I'm 75. That's 38 years from now.

So, I want you to think—just guesstimate it if you don't know exactly—how much longer do you plan on being in business?

Now with that number, think about the lifetime value of having those scripts done. How much money, additional income, would you make if you had those scripts done right now.

For me, I look at scripts as a 38-year value and I have a team of inside sales people. So, for me, it is millions of dollars. That's how important this is.

How much is it for you? Is the lifetime value $100,000? Is it $200,000? Is it

$1 million? Pick a number right now. Now I want you to imagine the money is rolling in. Your scripts are done and the money's rolling in.

You're making an extra $5,000 to $50,000 a month, just like Arvee Robinson. How is your life different? Are all your credit cards paid? Are you investing for retirement? Were you able to go down to the dealership and buy your dream car?

That was an amazing experience for me last year! I went down and bought a brand new BMW 7 Series and I never would have dreamed that I would have driven that car. Ten years ago I was driving a Mazda MX-3 that had gotten into an accident and was dented in the back. Now I get to drive my dream car. You can too.

Where will you live? Will you have a second home? What awards will you win for your salesmanship? Will you be able to retire your spouse? Where would you be able to send your kids to college?

Do you have parents that are getting ready to need your financial help? Do you just want to work a regular 40-hour work-week and you're working 50 to 60 hours right now and you just want to work 40 hours a week? How about, just take a one- or two-week vacation once a year with your family?

Sales scripting can make all of that come true for you. It's worked for me. It worked for Doug Bell, who I mentioned earlier, for Arvee Robinson.

It worked for Matt Asack. Some of you may know that name. He's one of my clients. He's a billionaire right now as a result of the scripts that I wrote for him.

Think about how your life will be different harnessing your skills. Think about this for a second: what if you never develop the sales script skills?

There's your life with the scripts, but then there's your life without the scripts. Think about what kind of result you would expect to produce without sales scripts.

If I took away sales scripting from me right now, I would have to take away a lot of dreams that I have. I have a dream to buy ten acres and build a campus where I can hold special trainings in Rocklin, California, where I live.

Without sales scripting I would even dare to dream that dream. How would I do it? There'd be no way to create the money. It's been fortunate that they don't require sales scripting as a prerequisite when training sales people because so many people out there never even come close to their potential. They achieve a fraction of their potential. They don't have the right tools.

You need to have the right tools in order to be successful at what you do. That's what these tools do for you. Once your scripts are done, you'll have them for the rest of your life. The sooner you get them done, the more sales you'll make. The longer you wait, the more sales you lose.

When do you think would be the best time to get your scripts done? Of course, the answer is 'as soon as possible.'

At this point in the call, I'm hopeful that you're open to embracing sales. You're open to embracing scripting and you've reached a point on this call right now and you go, "You know what? I want to learn how to get these scripts done just like Eric learned how to get them done."

I learned from Dr. Moine. Once I got how important it was—and there was no script writing boot camp that I could go to learn these skills in an ongoing program to support and develop my skills. The only place that had it was Dr. Moine and he charged a very high hourly rate.

Close Begins: Irresistible Offer

I realized how valuable it was and I said, "Heck! I'll put the money down to learn from him." and I'm so glad that I did.

Dr. Moine and I are coming together to do the boot camp of all boot camps. Two-day sales presentation boot camp, February 23rd and 24th at the LAX Marriott in Manhattan Beach.

So you fly into LAX, Los Angeles airport, just a couple miles away from where the hotel is; or you can drive in if you can drive there, and we're going to train you for two solid days.

What's going to happen during this boot camp—It's not just a boot camp. I'm going to give you my script-writing formulas. The exact way that I write a script—I'm going to teach you exactly how to do that so you have the formulas on how to create your sales scripts. We're training nine to five both days.

Here's a breakdown of the boot camp: Prior to the boot camp, we going to do a four-week teleseminar. The calls on Mondays at 2:00. These are four sessions on the phone to get you ready for the boot camp. Calls are on Monday at 2:00 and the first call was today.

Bringing the Benefits of the Teleseminar to Life

Now, here's the great news. You haven't sent in for the program yet so you weren't on the call and I recorded the call. So, tomorrow I'll send you the link and you can listen to the call that I did today for the prep work for the boot camp so you won't be behind.

The call was on identifying the benefits of your scripts. Remember earlier I talked about the components—that one of the components is the benefit?

Today I did a call just on benefits and then the homework assignment is to work on getting your benefits ready. You can listen to the recording of that tomorrow.

Then next Monday at two, I'm doing a call just on identifying the stories that you'll use. You can listen to that one live or the recording.

These are 2:00 California time.

Then the following Monday, we're doing a call on identifying the components of your close. I'm going to teach you my formula for how to write a close.

Then, the last Monday is on identifying the objections and the techniques on how to handle objections.

Bringing the Benefits of the Book Camp to Life

Then you come to boot camp and you're going to be trained for two days. The first day I'm going to train you on how to open your presentation. Opening is critical because oftentimes your prospects walk into the presentation with resistance because they view you as a salesperson and we've got to lower their resistance.

So I'm going to teach you how to open and how to build trust and rapport. Then how you create scripts to produce that.

In the second half of the first day is scripts on how to identify your prospect's needs and then we're going to go deep into story telling and how to use story scripts to overcome objections, bring the benefits to light, use stories to deepen the rapport with your prospect, use stories to influence your prospect on a sub-conscious level.

Then I'm going to teach you how to create your own customized script outline. Remember earlier in the call I gave you a very generic script outline? I want to teach you how to create your own customized script outline.

Second day, first half of the day, Dr. Moine. The world's greatest sales mind. He will be there live and in person. He will be teaching you his most powerful script-writing techniques. It's going to be incredible!

Second half of the day, all we're going to focus on, closing. We spending an entire half-day on closing.

Now, once the boot camp is done, you're going to need more support. I worked with Dr. Moine on an ongoing basis. You're going to need more support. So, with this program, I've got a special for you tonight to give you the support that you need.

We're going to do a four-week teleseminar after the boot camp's done to get you into action and these will be on Mondays at two also and then all the calls are recorded.

Call Number One is you're going to set your script-writing goal. You're going to get your outline done and you're going to get your close done.

Then, the following Monday, you're going to pick the stories that you're going to tell, you're going to identify the benefits that you're going to communicate and then where in your presentation you're going to deliver those.

Then the following week, you're going to work on your opening and your probing questions. This Call Four is putting it all together.

So, it's eight calls and then two days of training.

Price

The investment for the program is $1,995. So it's just a shade under $2,000. Now, I feel really great about offering you this program for just a shade under $2,000, because keep in mind Loral Langemeier, when she hired me and put me on her team, it was $5,000 up front and there was an ongoing fee. She invested about $50,000 with me.

Contrast

When I hired Dr. Moine it was $30,000. So, I'm going to train you and give you my entire system for just a shade under $2,000.

I put together a very special offer for all of you on the call tonight. We're going to do something really, really special and I have an irresistible offer for you. I'm going to make it really, really easy for you to say "yes."

So, here's what we're going to do for you. For those of you that register in the next hour I'm going to have my staff in the office right now—and they're there to take your call or you can register on the internet, whatever you prefer—those of you that register in the next hour, I'm going to allow you to participate in my scriptwriting club.

Bonus

In my scriptwriting club the investment is $2,000 for that. With the scriptwriting club you get a lifetime membership to the club; so you never have to make another investment in this club ever again and the benefits are you can repeat the sales presentation boot camp as often as you want for life.

So, let's say that in three months, we have another one coming up, you want to come back, you've got to repeat the course; and you don't have to make another investment. You can come as my guest.

We had some folks come to my last sales presentation boot camp in December and then we announced this one coming up here in February, the 23rd and 24th, and several of the people that attended in December were also part of the scriptwriting club, they're able to repeat the course and they don't have to pay for it! They're going to get trained by Dr. Moine for free!

Okay, so you can repeat the sales presentation boot camp, register in the next hour and then the conference calls that I'm inviting you to—I'm going to be doing several of those in the future—and those are invitation only—and you're going to be invited to future script-writing conference calls that you can plug into live or the recording and you can access those training calls for life.

So, when I learn new things and I put together special script-writing conference calls with these new ideas that I'm learning, you can come back and listen to those calls and you never have to invest in it ever again. So we're going to give that to you for free for signing up in the next hour.

Guarantee

The program comes with a one hundred percent money back guarantee and the guarantee is awesome. Here's how it works. Go through the conference calls, the entire two-day boot camp, get all of my distinctions, get Dr. Moine's training, get the manual, get my entire system on script-writing, if you are not certain that this is going to transform your life financially, it's a one hundred percent money back guarantee.

Because some of you that are listening to me right now might be thinking, "This sounds great and it has to work. If I go to this boot camp and I invest this $2,000, it has to work. There is no other option. Where I'm at financially, it has to work."

And if you're in that place—I've been there before. I can relate with that—and if you're in that place, I understand, that's why we offer our 100% money back guarantee—no questions asked.

Call to Action

What we're going to do for you also—those of you that register in the next hour—is we're going to give you a $700 discount, making your total investment only $1,295.

For my entire scriptwriting system, all the conference calls, the scriptwriting club, the lifetime membership, training by Dr. Moine, to give you the real tools, the skill that's been holding you back from your greatness.

Once I got script writing, I went from almost being fired to top producer and you will have similar results. You will have a transformation in your ability to clearly communicate your offer to your prospects and we're going to be able to deliver that to you. You're going to get the finest training in the world for a one-time investment of $1,295. Of course this is tax deductible in your business.

There are two ways to register. The first way is I put up a very special page on my website and the only way to get this special offer is you have to go to this specific page because it's not part of the main website, and it's www.ericlofholm.com/salesbootcamp and you can pay with any major credit or debit card, Visa, American Express, MasterCard or Discover.

My staff is also in the office. I asked a few people to stay late and the number to call is either 888.81.SALES, that's 888.817.2537 Or you can call international 916.435.0416.

Double Close

I'm going to do something extra-special for the first ten people who register. I have a sales scripting one-hour DVD. It's absolutely awesome. It comes with a DVD and an audio CD and it retails for $99. So, for the first ten people who register, I'm going to give you that DVD at no charge AND I have a special scripting report. It outlines 77 different sales scripting techniques and I'll send that out to you prior to the boot camp and that special report goes for $99. It's the only script writing special report of it's kind that I'm aware of in the world. It is absolutely awesome! Full of 77 powerful ideas!

For the first ten, I'm also going to include that AND, last year I did a script-writing teleseminar. It was eight weeks. It was awesome! People paid $697 to do that eight-week course with me and I recorded it.

So for the first ten people who register online, on the website, or call the number and again, the website is **www.ericlofholm.com/salesbootcamp** OR call my office at 888.81.SALES, that's 888.817.2537, or 916.435.0416. The first ten people are going to get this awesome scripting DVD and audio CD. This $99 special report. It's an awesome report!

And I'm going to give you the recordings of this class that I did, this tele-seminar, where people invested $697. It's an eight-week course. We're going to give that to the first ten people who register.

I have a couple of final thoughts for you to wrap up.

I want to acknowledge you for being a winner because only a winner would be on this call. You have a desire to increase your results and possibly to make 2008 your best year ever. I acknowledge you for being on this call and I want you to pat yourself on the back right now for being on the call.

I know that many of you have already gone on the website and you're signing up right now or your calling in my office right now registering, and I also know there are still some people on the call and you want to do it but you're just not quite sure. You're right on the fence.

I understand. Because, you're like, "It has to work to for me."

Let me ask you a question. Worst-case scenario—let's say you come to the boot camp, what's the worst-case scenario? You come to the boot camp, you get two days of awesome training from Dr. Moine and myself. You come to the pro-gram and your worst-case scenario is you don't feel that this is the right program for you.

You go through the entire training and you don't feel it's the right program and you come to me and say, "Eric, I tried it out and it's just not the right pro-gram." Worst case scenario is you get your money back.

Okay, now let's look at the best-case scenario. The best-case scenario is that this is the missing piece for you—you see you're already motivated. You've got a great product or service. You just need the right words and this becomes the missing piece for you.

Just like Joey Aszterbaum, you become Number One in your company or you become a millionaire or you eliminate your credit card debt 100% or whatever is important to you, your life changes forever.

I want you to know with every ounce of my being that that is absolutely possible for you! This program is that powerful. I am that powerful. Dr. Moine is that powerful. The information is that powerful—to truly change your life.

All you need to do right now is get on the internet, go to **ericlofholm.com/salesbootcamp**, or pick up the phone right now; hang up from me right now, pick up the phone call 888.81.SALES, 916.435.0416. Take action! Let this year be your best year ever! You want it to be your best year ever! This is what's going to be different for you. You're going to come to the boot camp and it's going to change your life.

Thank you for calling in. I am thrilled that you were with me tonight and allowed me the opportunity to share this value with you about sales scripting. I wish you the best of success this year!

Have a great rest of your evening. Talk to you later. Bye-bye.

Bonus Chapter #7

Sample Local Talk Script

Good morning!

[Let them respond.]

My name is _____ [say your name].

I am a sales trainer with Eric Lofholm International. We have been helping salespeople and sales managers increase their sales results for over nine years [say network marketing to MLM groups].

Our mission is to help people make more sales. How many of you by a show of hands would like to make more sales?

All of you because we all make more money when we make more sales.

Now money is not everything but would you all agree that cash flow does solve a lot of problems?

How many of you believe that you have potential inside of you to perform at a higher level than the level you are currently performing at?

I brought this pen with me and I would like to do a quick demonstration.

In a moment I am going to let go of pen. The pen is going to do one of three things. It is either going rise to the ceiling, stay suspended in mid air, or fall to the ground.

What do you think is going to happen?

Let's test it out and see what happens. [Drop the book.]

If you guessed the pen was going to fall to the ground you were right. Every time I have ever done the demonstration the pen has always fallen to the ground because of the law of gravity.

There are universal principles of success and selling that when you apply them you will see immediate increases in your results. How many of you knew before I got here today that there are principles that when applied will increase your results? [Lead the audience by raising your hand.]

What our company does is teach those universal principles to people like you.

I would like to share with you a little background on the president of our company Eric Lofholm.

Eric started off as a sales failure. At the end of his first year he was written up for missing quota two months in row. They threatened to fire him if he missed quota one more time. It was at this time that Eric met his sales mentor, Dr. Donald Moine. Dr. Moine is the author of Unlimited Selling Power. With Dr. Moine help and ideas Eric hit quota. The quota was $10,000. Eric did $10,500. The next month he did $51,000 and seven months later he did $160,000. Jot this down in your notes. Selling is a learned skill.

Eric then started sharing what was working for him with his co-workers. Many of them took the ideas Eric shared with them and their sales results went up. Eric realized that teaching sales skills came very easily to him and more importantly his students were able to easily understand what he was teaching and then become better salespeople.

Over nine years ago Eric started Eric Lofholm International out of a spare bedroom in his Condo. We have grown to a company that has a staff of over 30 people and over 10,000 clients all over the world.

Insert a brief story here about how we met and why you are a part of Eric Lofholm International.

I have two outcomes for our meeting today. My first outcome is to share some great ideas with you. My second outcome is to invite you to participate in our one year sales mentor program. At the end of our meeting I will give you all the details on that program.

[What is important here is to cover one, two, or three content points and then do the Level 10 exercise. You can do baseling strategy, closing, POI, referrals, etc. Always do the Level 10 exercise before the close and deliver the close as close to word-for-word as possible.]

There are three ways to elevate your sales results. Jot this down in your notes.

- The Inner Game
- The Outer Game
- Action
- The Inner Game is the mental side of success.
- It is your belief systems.
- It is your comfort zone.
- It is how you deal with fear of rejection.
- The outer game is the tactical side of success.
- In selling it is what you say, when you say it, how you say it.
- The third component is action.
- Moving yourself to follow through and take action.
- Now between inner game and outer game which one to you think is more important?
- That is right the inner game.

[If they want a customized meeting on any topic lead with two ideas on that topic. For example if they want the meeting to focus on prospecting you could lead with talking about consistency and mindset. This should be three to five minutes of the workshop. If they want a customized workshop on prospecting you will simply change the content below from baseline to prospecting baseline.]

The next idea I would like to share with you is called the baseline strategy. Go ahead and jot those two words down in your notes.

Each of you has a baseline in terms of the results you are producing on a monthly basis. I know one of the ways you measure results is _____ [use terms that they would use in their industry like, recruits, units, transactions, or income] Let's say someone here was averaging _____ per month. Your baseline would be _____. The baseline is everything that you are currently doing to produce two. The number of calls you make, your time management, your goal setting, your selling skills. It is everything.

The baseline strategy is to keep doing what you have been doing because it is producing a positive result. Then add one new idea or one new strategy thus you will be able to produce a greater result.

Part of the purpose of the subconscious mind is to answer whatever question you ask it. Ask yourself right now what is one thing you could add to your baseline to increase your results. Whatever answer you get write it down.

Go around the room and have people share what their answers were.

Stories that you can tell related to baseline are:

One of our clients is a loan officer in Hemet. His name is Joey Aszterbaum. Eric met Joey in a workshop just like this. Prior to meeting Eric Joey's best month was around $10,000 in income. Joey, with Eric's help added about 30 things to his baseline. Here are a few:

> Consistent post card marketing to realtors and his refinance clients.
>
> Tracking results daily
>
> He turned his web site into a lead generation machine.
>
> He improved at handling the common objections that come up.

There were many other things Joey did as well.

As a result Joey, within six months of joining our program had a $30,000 income month. Not only that but the ideas that he has learned he will be able to benefit from for the rest of his life. It is possible Joey will earn several hundred thousand dollars in increased income as a result of what he has learned from Eric.

Joey has done so well that he now has his own billboard in Hemet and he just closed on his first real estate investment property.

Eric met Eric and Deva Edelman in a workshop just like this. They had been realtors for about six months. Have you ever heard don't expect to make much money your first year in residential real estate. They joined Eric's program and added several things to their baseline. Here are a few:

> They started teaching real estate seminars to first time home buyers.
>
> They improved their web site.
>
> They become more consistent in their prospecting.

There were many other things they did with Eric's help as well.

As a result they were named realtor of the month their 12 months as realtors in an office of about 40 realtors. They received this award because they closed five transactions in 30 days. They made around $40,000 that month. What is even more exciting though is they will be able to benefit from the ideas for the next 20 years.

Modeling Chunk

[If they want something customized on prospecting you will substitute modeling with whom could you model that is great at prospecting.]

The next idea we are going to talk about today is modeling. The modeling principle is if someone else is producing a result if you do what they do then you will produce a similar result.

Don't reinvent the wheel.

Don't reinvent the wheel.

Don't reinvent the wheel.

Having said that what does everyone what to do?

Let them respond reinvent the wheel.

It is interesting. It is like people have this creative side that they feel they need to express. Here is a very profound quote for I would like you to write down.

The most inefficient way of learning is experience.

Let's do a quick exercise.

Write down who is one person you would model and what would you model about them?

Go around the room and have people share.

Referral Script

Are referrals an important part of your business? [Let them respond.] They are a very important part of my business as well. I am going to share with you a couple of great referral ideas while asking you for referrals as well.

The most important idea regarding referrals is to have a referral system. Here is our system. Take out the referral sheet that I gave all of you at the beginning of the workshop. A good referral for me is a sales manager with a team of six or more people in San Diego. When you think of a good referral think of other offices that your company has, where you have worked in the past, and where your clients work. Industries that we work in addition to yours are: real estate, mortgage, car dealerships, network marketing, and insurance. We help anyone who is in commissioned sales.

If you can help me out today with three or more referrals I will give you this free CD today.

So our system is we hand out the form, we educate our clients on what a good referral is, we offer an incentive and we ask.

Please jot those four ideas in your notes:

1. Form

2. Educate

3. Incentive

4. Ask

That is our system. Does it work? Well we have received over 10,000 referrals that have resulted in hundreds of thousands of dollars in sales.

What Level Exercise

[If they want the meeting customized on prospecting they instead of saying, "What level have you been playing at over the last 30 days?", lead with, "What level have you been playing at in prospecting?"]

The last exercise we are going to do is called "What level am I playing at?" Go ahead and jot that down in your notes.

Here is how the exercise works. I am going to say good morning. You are going to respond back good morning at a Level 6.

Okay, let's give it a try. Good morning.

Very good. So that was a 6. Let's try it again. Except this time we are going to play at an 8. If some of you want to smile this time that is fine.

Good morning! [Say it a little louder with a little more energy.]

That was great. You are the best group I have had all morning. We are going to try this one last time. This time we are going to play at a 10. I want you to give it everything you've got.

GOOD MORNING, EVERYONE! [Say it a little louder with a little more energy.]

Give yourselves a hand. That was great. The first time we did the exercise it was a 6. The last time we did it, it was a 10. The first time it was a 6 and the last time it was a 10 [yes, repeat the phrase]. My question for all of you is this: over the last 30 days as you have been coming to work on a daily basis, what level have you been playing at? What level have you been playing at in referrals? What level have you been playing at in time management?

My belief is you get out of life what it is that you put into it and all the rewards are for those that play full out. And who decides what level we play at as human beings? That is right, we do. If you would like to produce the best results you have ever produced you must get yourself to do two things. Take some new action and get out of your comfort zone.

If you would like to produce the best results you have ever produced you must get yourself to do two things. Take some new action and get out of your comfort zone. One action you all have the opportunity to take is to participate in our Protege Program.

In the Protege Program you will receive all of the tools and resources you need to take your career to the next level.

All Eric asks for is 30 minutes per week. And you can pick when you spend the 30 minutes. There are two ways to learn. On one hand is to learn these ideas and techniques on your own. On the other hand you can learn from an expert. How many of you would agree the fastest, easiest way to learn is to learn from an expert? [Raise your hand.]

Each week Eric will share with you 30 minutes of his best ideas on one area of sales and success. The live calls are every Thursday from 4:00 to 4:30. From 4:30 to 5:00 the call is an interactive electronic question and answer call. What that means is participants email in their questions and Eric answers them live on the call. Each call is recorded and the notes will be sent to you via email. Every week there is a new topic and every Friday the recording of the call is delivered directly to your desktop on your computer. It is sent to a software program called iTunes. If you don't have iTunes it's free. The call will be on your computer available for you to listen whenever you want. The program is going to help you with your focus, your motivation and you will learn how to sell from honesty, integrity and compassion.

Here is what you are going to learn during the program:

1. How to set unlimited appointments—how many of you just need more leads or appointments to have an income breakthrough by a show of hands?

2. How to consistently close sale after sale—how many of you would like to have more confidence on every sales presentation for the rest of your life by a show of hands?

3. How to handle every objection—how many of you would like to be able to confidently handle any objection and not feel pushy or sales by show of hands?

4. How to break out of your income comfort zone—how many of you would like to learn how to eliminate yo-yo income months and achieve the income of your dreams month after month, year after year by a show of hands?

5. How to get yourself to take action—some of you in the room if you could just get yourself to take more action could double your sales.

If you improve in any of these areas what will happen to your income? [They will say they will go up.]

By participating in the program you will improve in all of these areas. All you need to know about the program is it will help you increase your income for life. And how many of you by a show of hands would like to increase your income for the rest of your life?

[Hand out forms.]

What is the first thing that you notice on the form? [Pause and let them answer.]

That is right $1,295. Now sometimes when I share with people the investment they say _____ [say your name], $1,295 is a lot of money. And I guess on one hand it is a lot of money. $1,295 is $1,295 no matter how you slice it but let me ask you this question…If the program can help you truly perform at a higher level for the rest of your career would you agree that $1,295 is a very small amount of money yes, or yes. [Pause.]

As a bonus for signing up today you will receive:

You will also receive four hours of Eric's best ideas on DVD. This is a $149 dollar value. This is another way for you to learn.

You will also receive Eric's Persuasion and Influence System on audio CD. The audio CD program contains eight hours of Eric's best ideas. It contains Eric's complete system. The program also comes with a workbook. This is a $199 value.

In total you will receive over $348 in bonuses by signing up today.

We will also guarantee your success in the program. If after 30 days you are not satisfied for any reason we will refund you tuition 100%, no questions asked.

At our company we believe in rewarding people who take action. Those of you who sign up today in the Protege Program we are going to offer you a $800 discount making your total investment only $495. That includes over $348 in bonuses.

We have two ways you can register.

You can sign up for a 1-year membership for $495 or a lifetime membership for $695. [You can also offer $149 down and $50 per month as a monthly subscription. If there is company support say it here. For example.: "Now I spoke with Bob before the meeting. He has agreed to reimburse you back 1/2 on the close of your next escrow. At $495 this was a great deal. At $250 this is the biggest no brainer in the history of sales training."]

On your forms where it says $1,295 cross out $1,295 and write down $495 for 1 year, $695 for lifetime.

Your total investment if you enroll today is $495 for 1 year and $695 for lifetime. [If you offer the monthly subscription, I would offer the 1 year or the monthly; I would not offer the lifetime membership.]

Where is asks for your name go ahead and jot down your name. Put down your company name. Jot down your mailing address. Jot down your email. Jot down your home phone, work phone, and cell phone.

You can pay with any major credit card, Visa, American Express, Master Card or Discover. We also accept personal checks or cash.

Does anyone have any questions about the program?

If anyone is on the fence about signing up I want to encourage you to try out the program because the universe rewards people who take action differently than those who don't.

The last thing I want to share with you is this. I didn't come to the meeting today to twist your arm and tell you that you need to sign up for this program. How many of you in this room already knew you could benefit from getting more sales training by a show of hands. That is right. Because there is only one person in this room who knows if you could benefit from this program and who is that? [Pause.] That is right: yourself. I want to strongly encourage you to take action and sign up now.

I want to thank you for being a great group.

If anyone needs to go to their desk or car to get a check or credit card go ahead and do that now.

Sample Appointment Setting Script

Appointment Setting Ideas

1. The purpose of setting the appointment is to set the appointment.
2. There are stand alone benefits to the appointment that are different than the benefits of your speech.
3. Always ask for the appointment and be silent.
4. Request appointments using email.
5. Have an appointment setting goal for each month.
6. Have an angle as to why they should let you speak to their group.

Appointment Setting Script

Receptionist says:

> Thank you for calling XYZ Company, how may I direct your call?
>
> Who would I speak with in regards to being a guest speaker at your office?

You would need to speak with Bob Jones. [Write down Bob's name on an index card so the next time you call in you have the lead prospected.]

Is Bob in?

Hi Bob, how are you today? [Let them respond.]

My name is _____. My company is Eric Lofholm International. We are a California-based sales training firm. The reason for the call today is to offer you a complimentary 30- to 45-minute sales training on the topic of your choice. The training is free, very motivational and everyone will be able to get at least one idea they can immediately implement to increase their results.

What we get out of the free workshop is 3 to 5 minutes at the end to let your team know about one of our sales training programs.

How do you feel about me speaking to your team?

If they say yes say, when do you normally have your meetings?

Great, I am open on Tuesday the 9th or Tuesday the 16th at 4:00. What would work best for you?

Once you have a date and time say:

You will receive an email confirmation within 24 hours. About 1 week prior to the workshop I will be calling you to customize the training for you.

Conference Call Setting Script

Is Bob in?

Hi Bob, how are you today? [Let them respond.]

My name is Eric Lofholm. My company is Eric Lofholm International. We are a global sales training firm. The reason for the call today is to offer you a sales training conference call for your team at a time that is convenient for you. Here is how it works.

The call is free. I can customize it to the topic of your choice. Popular topics include time management, objection handling, closing, and referrals.

We can use my bridge line to do the call or a speaker phone in your office.

The reason I am willing to do it for free is it is a creative way for me to get new clients. At the end of the call I will introduce one of my sales training home study courses to your team. Anyone that is interested can call my office to order. How do you feel about me speaking to your team?

[If they say "Yes", say:] What day of the week and time would work best for you?

Great, I am open on Tuesday the 9th or Tuesday the 16th at 4. What would work best for you?

[Once you have a date and time say:]

You will receive an email confirmation within 24 hours. About 1 week prior to the conference call I will be calling you to customize the training for you.

Appointment Setting Template

Get the name of the decision maker.

Tell them who you are.

Explain "The Deal"

Ask for the conference call or speech

Alternate Template

This is who I am.

This is why I am calling.

This is what I would like to do.

Would you like to do it?

Different Ways to Structure the "Deal"

Value add to the person you are doing the call for.

You can do a call or speech for a group that adds stand alone value. In this case the value you are bringing is the talk itself.

50/50

In this case you are splitting the revenue 50/50. You can also do 70/30 or 45/55, etc. Also, sometimes the split doesn't happen until after credit card processing fees are taken out.

Conference Call Swap

In this case you would do a conference call for them and they would do a conference call for you.

Marketing Swap

In this case they would promote your conference call or speech and you would provide some type of marketing benefit for them.

Favor

In many cases people will help you if you simply ask them as a favor to promote your call or talk.

When does the money get paid?

The money is paid whenever you agree to pay the money and when the person actually pays. Typically the money is paid out in 30 days or less.

Bonus Chapter #9

Sample Scripts for Coaches

Many of my students earn money coaching, either as one of my sales trainers or running their own coaching business. Here are a few scripts you can use to grow your coaching practice.

Coaching Appointment Setting Script

One of the best ways to generate cash in the speaking business is to coach clients one-on-one. The best way I have found to set up coaching appointments is to offer a complimentary coaching session when I speak or do conference calls.

There are two ways to do this.

The first way is to offer the coaching session at the end of your presentation. You would do this if you were not selling something during your talk.

The second way is to offer the coaching session during the middle of your presentation. You would do this if you were selling something at the end of the presentation. The reason to offer the coaching session in the middle is the confused mind doesn't buy. You don't want to have two offers at the end of the presentation.

When offering a complimentary coaching session during a speech, use a half sheet or full sheet of paper as the appointment setting form.

When offering a complimentary coaching session via email or conference calls, use a web form, email, and/or phone number for the client to request the session.

Speaking/Conference Call Script

What I would like to do is spend a few minutes with you and share with you how it works.

I gave all of you a half sheet. It looks like this. [Hold up the half sheet.] Take a moment and find your half sheet.

Olympic athletes all have one thing in common. Do you know what it is? [Let them respond.]

That is right: a coach.

How many of you would agree by a show of hands that you would be more likely to follow through on your goals and commitments if you were working with a coach? [Lead them by raising your hand.]

That is exactly why I offer my coaching program. To help people like you achieve at your best.

The free coaching session will last for 30 minutes.

During the call we will get to know each other better and you will get an experience of coaching.

At the end of the call I will share with you how my ongoing coaching program works.

There is no cost or obligation to purchase coaching.

Take a moment right now and where it asks for your name jot your name down.

Where it asks for you phone number jot down the best number to reach you at.

And where it asks for your email jot down you email address.

Has everyone completed their form that would like a free coaching session?

Great. Take a moment and pass your coaching forms to the center. Those of you who filled out a form will receive a call from my office in the next day to set up your coaching call.

Coaching Appointment Setting Script

Hi is _____ in?

Hi _____. This is _____ [your name] calling from _____ [your company]. How are you today? [Let them respond.]

Great, the reason for the call is you requested a complimentary coaching session with me when you saw me speak last Tuesday [or, "you responded to the email I sent out about the complimentary coaching session."]

I do coaching session between 10:00 and 4:00 Monday through Friday [or whatever your schedule is]. Do mornings or afternoons work best for you? [Let them respond.]

Great, I have an opening on Tuesday, September 12 at 3:00. Does that work for you?

To prepare for the call I would like you to think about three things you would like to improve in your sales. [Fill in what you do].

I will be calling you on Tuesday, September 12 at 3:00. Which number would you like me to call you at? [Let them respond.]

I would like to send you over an email confirmation. Which email address would you like me to use? [Get email address and send them a confirmation.]

Get Coaching Clients Script

One-on-one coaching is one of the best ways to create cash flow.

The best way I have found to get clients is audition for them. Below is a script I have used over and over again to get coaching clients.

Converting Leads to Clients

Is there any thing in particular you would like us to cover today?

[Let them respond.]

What do you sell?

How long have you been selling it?

What are two or three of your strengths?

On what do you feel you need to work?

If you could make progress toward any three goals over the next six months, what would they be?

What would be the benefit to you if you made progress on each of those goals?

[Share some coaching tips with them.]

What I would like to do now is spend a few minutes with you and let you know how my coaching program works.

Do you believe by working with a coach, you would be more likely to follow through on your goals and commitments?

[Let them respond.]

Here is how my coaching program works.

The price of the program is $250 per month or $500 per month.

For $250 you would receive two 30-minute calls.

For $500 you would receive four 30-minute calls.

The maximum number of clients I work with is 20. In addition to coaching, I also speak and run my business.

I guarantee the program is going to help you. The way the guarantee works is after 30 days, if you are not 100% satisfied, I will give you a full refund. At the end of 30 days the program goes month-to-month. You can stay in the program as long as you are receiving benefit.

Would you like to be one of the 20 clients with whom I work?

[If they say, "Yes," continue. If they say, "No," wrap up the call. I do not believe in overcoming objections with coaching clients. I believe in working with people that are eager and ready to learn. Not with ones who need to be pushed.]

Would you like to have two calls or four calls per month?

You can pay month to month or if you prepay three months you will receive the 4th month at no charge. What would work best for you? We accept all major credit cards. Which credit card would you like to use?

Selling a Boot Camp from the Front of the Room

Syntax

Intro

Outcomes

Your Story

Chunk 1

Share a success story that reinforces the point where the client purchased the product you are offering.

Chunk 2

Share a success story that reinforces the point where the client purchased the product you are offering.

Chunk 3

Share a success story that reinforces the point where the client purchased the product you are offering.

Call to Action

- Use scarcity.
- You must get the audience to like you (use humor).
- Close them in their seats or drive them to the back table.
- Irresistible offer.
- In almost every case use a price drop.
- Option 1: Give the price and then offer bonuses and a price break for taking action now

- Option 2: Bundle the bonuses and the product and sell as a package then offer a price break for taking action today.

Tips

- People will buy today if you give them a reason to buy today.
- In preparing your script make the following laundry lists:
  - Benefits.
  - Stories.
  - Offer.
  - Objections.
- When telling stories share where the client was before they started working with you, what product they bought, and where they are now.
  - I like PowerPoint photos to take up the entire PowerPoint slide.
  - Sales mindset.
  - Selling equals service.
  - When you sell, sell from honesty, integrity, and compassion.
  - Selling is about leading.
  - Selling is about moving people to action.
- Below is the wording on from the PowerPoint for promoting this program that went with this sample script.

How to Sell Information Products, Seminars, Boot Camp, and Coaching Programs, and Generate Leads, and Book Appointments Using Sales Scripts Mentor Program

8 Week Teleseminar + Script Templates

Copies of my scripts
Sales Scripting Boot Camp
Lifetime Membership to Script Writing Club
October 11-12
Saturday & Sunday
Westin South Coast Plaza
Costa Mesa, California
9-5 both days

You will learn:

- How to create a customized sales script that closes
- My script writing formula
- Over 50 sales scripting techniques
- How to create customized objection responses
- How to create a customized referral script to get unlimited referrals
- You will have all of these skills for life

4 Week Teleseminar

- Call 1 Set Your Goal—Outline—Close
- Call 2 Identify Stories—Identify Benefits
- Call 3 Opening—Probing Questions
- Call 4 Put is All Together

Script Writing Club

- Lifetime Membership into the Script Writing Club
- Repeat the Sales Scripting Boot Camp as often as you want for life
- Access to numerous bonus script writing conference calls and podcasts
- Each call comes with a template (my script if applicable)

8 Week Teleseminar

- Call 1 Appointment Setting Script
- Call 2 Free Local Talk Script
- Call 3 Conference Call Script
- Call 4 Coaching Appointment Setting
- Call 5 Coaching Enrollment Script
- Call 6 Sell a Boot Camp or Product Front of the Room Script
- Call 7 Sell a Boot Camp over the Phone Script
- Call 8 Follow up with non-buyers Script

What is included:

- 8 Week Teleseminar + Script Templates- $1,995
- Copies of my scripts—$5,000
- Script Boot Camp—$1,995 (bring assistant/spouse)
- Lifetime Membership to Script Writing Club- $2,000 Value
- CD Set (first 30)—$99
- Coaching Session (first 30)—$250
- $11,349 Total Value
- 30 Day Money Back Guarantee

Try the program for 30 days. If you are unhappy for any reason we will refund your tuition 100%

Your total investment today is $995

Sample Phone Sales Script for Selling a Product or Service

Hi is _____ in?

Hi _____. This is _____ from Eric Lofholm's office. How are you today?

Great. The reason for the call is you expressed interest in our script writing training. I am calling to set up a time to go over the details with you. If you have 20 minutes now we can speak now or we can schedule a time. What works best for you?

Hi is _____ in?

Hi _____. This is _____ from Eric Lofholm's office. I am calling for our scheduled call. Are you ready for our call?

Here is how our call is going to go today. I am going to give you a brief overview of how we help people with our Script Writing Academy. Then I am going to ask you some questions. And then at the end of the call I will give you all the details about the upcoming program. Sound good?

If you are familiar with Eric Lofholm's story then you know he went from a bottom producer to a top producer with he mentor, Dr. Moine's help. What you may not know is what Dr. Moine worked with Eric on was his sales presentation skills. Eric has made a small fortune by mastering his sales script. In our Script

Writing Academy Eric will train you on how to develop a great sales presentation. Once you have it complete you will have it for the rest of your life.

When we talk about a sales presentation we also mean a sales script.

The definition of a sales script is simply words in sequence that have meaning. So a sales script is simply preparing your presentation to deliver a powerful, persuasive, effective presentation that moves people to action because that is what you want isn't it? [Let them say yes.] Great!

Let's talk about you and your business for a few minutes.

What do you sell?

How long have you been doing it?

Do you have a written sales script?

Where do you feel you need to improve the most in your presentation?

There are several different types of sales scripts. Here are a few:

- Main presentation
- Appointment setting
- Referrals
- Front of the room
- Conference calls
- Objection handling
- Follow up
- Recruiting

And then each product needs a script.

Which scripts do you need?

Imagine these scripts are now done. How much more would you expect to make in the next 12 months?

Once the scripts are done you will be able to benefit from these scripts for the rest of your life. What would you expect the lifetime value to be?

Imagine the scripts are done and the money is rolling in. How would your life be different?

Would you be driving the same car you are currently driving?

Would you live in the same home you are currently living in?

What else would be different?

Let me share some success stories with you so you can really get the impact of how an effective sales script/sales presentation can impact your life.

Eric was about to be fired from his job 15 years ago mostly because he didn't have an effective sales presentation. With Dr. Moine's help Eric created a great presentation that took Eric from worst to first in 30 days. He is still using the techniques 15 years later. Once you learn the techniques you have them forever. Would you like Eric to teach you how to create a great sales presentation? [Let them say yes.]

Great. Arvee Robinson wanted the same thing. Arvee is a coach and speakers. She was struggling with enrolling people in her coaching program because she had a bad presentation. Arvee put Eric on her team. Eric taught her how to create a great presentation. Arvee now has a full practice and she doubled her fees. Arvee recently purchased a home because of her increase in sales that was directly related to Eric's teachings. What is great for Arvee is she has the script for the rest of her life. The script will make Arvee over $500,000 in coaching fees.

Cher Cunningham sells timeshares on the resale marketing. She had over a $500,000 in orders on one of her resorts but she had no inventory. She used Eric's scripting techniques to create the inventory by influencing people who owned timeshares that had no plan of selling them to sell at her price. She then immediately sold them to her waiting buyers. She bought and sold 16 units in one month. The real estate agent on the transaction made over $60,000 in one month.

Eric and Deva Edelman had been real estate agents for six months. Eric taught them how to create a great listing presentation. He also taught them how to create an appointment setting script, referral scripts and negotiation scripts. They sold five deals in their 12 months of being realtors. They got real estate agent of the month and earned nearly $40,000 in a single month.

When best selling author Loral Langemeier was starting her telemarketing team she turned to Eric for help. Loral put Eric on her team. Eric helped Loral with scripts for her back end telemarketers. Their sales results went from under $100,000 per month to over $1,000,000 per month.

J.W. Hermes sells vacation ownership for the Westin in Maui. J.W. was struggling in sales when he met Eric. Eric taught him how to create a great sales presentation. Less than 18 months later J.W. set the all-time company sales record making over $1,000,000 in sales in a single month.

Once your scripts are done, you will have them for the rest of your life. The sooner you get them done, the more sales you will make. The longer you wait the more sales you will lose. When do you think it would be the best time to get your scripts done? [Let them respond.]

There are two ways you can get your scripts done. You can do it on your own or your can have Eric's help. What do you think is the fastest, easiest way for you to get your scripts done?

How many more years do you plan on benefiting from the scripts?

By planning on being in business for at least 10 years you can put Eric on your team for less than $100 per year which is less than 33 cents per day.

I am so excited to be able to offer you our Script Writing Academy.

There is no training program or seminar in the world like this program. Eric is one of the best script writers in the world. He will be sharing with you his proven formulas so you can incorporate them into your scripts.

Script Writing Academy
Sales Scripting Boot Camp

October 11-12

Saturday & Sunday

Westin South Coast Plaza

686 Anton Blvd

Costa Mesa, CA

9-5 both days

You will learn:

- How to create a customized sales script that closes
- My script writing formula
- Over 50 sales scripting techniques
- How to create customized objection responses

- How to create a customized referral script to get unlimited referrals
- You will have all of these skills for life

What will be covered

- How to create your outline
- How to identify your sales model
- How to use story scripts to overcome objections, bring the benefits to life, use stories to deepen the rapport with your prospect, use stories to influence your prospect on a subconscious level
- Objection handling
- Closing
- Putting it all together

Dr. Moine will be there for 1 day on Sunday training

Program is limited to 100 people.
Teleseminar

4 Week Teleseminar

- Call 1 Set Your Goal—Outline—Close
- Call 2 Identify Stories—Identify Benefits
- Call 3 Opening—Probing Questions
- Call 4 Put is All Together

Script Writing Club

- Lifetime Membership into the Script Writing Club
- Repeat the Sales Scripting Boot Camp as often as you want for life
- Access to numerous bonus script writing conference calls and podcasts

---

What is included:

1. Eric Lofholm Scripting Boot Camp- $1,995
2. Script Writing Club Membership—$2,000
3. Teleseminar—$495

$4,480 Total Value

Guarantee

Your total investment today is

- $995
- $1,495 for 2

My Success Journal Notes

Use the following blank pages to declare your success intention and record the best ideas you learn from each chapter. As you learn and take action, identify the ten best ideas you're learning and, applying the 80/20 rule, focus on applying those ideas one at a time to improving your sales results and business performance.

Success Intention:

I, _____ declare my intention to succeed at sales by studying this book and applying its ideas.

_____ Date

(After filling in your intention, let me know by sending me an email with the subject line "Success intention" at **wins@ericlofholm.com**!)

Notes:
Introduction

Notes:
Part I: The Inner Game of Sales Scripting

_____

_____

_____

_____

_____

_____

_____

_____

_____

_____

_____

_____

_____

_____

_____

_____

_____

_____

_____

_____

_____

_____

_____

_____

_____

_____

_____

Notes:
Chapter 1: Who's Afraid of Scripting?
Getting Past Fear of Sounding Scripted

_____

_____

_____

_____

_____

_____

_____

_____

_____

_____

_____

_____

_____

_____

_____

_____

_____

_____

_____

_____

_____

_____

Notes:
Chapter 2: Breaking through Scriptwriter's Block

_____

_____

_____

_____

_____

_____

_____

_____

_____

_____

_____

_____

_____

_____

_____

_____

_____

_____

_____

_____

_____

_____

_____

_____

_____

Notes:
Part II: The Outer Game of Sales Scripting

Notes:
Chapter 3: The Scripting Process

_____

_____

_____

_____

_____

_____

_____

_____

_____

_____

_____

_____

_____

_____

_____

_____

_____

_____

_____

_____

_____

_____

_____

_____

Notes:
Chapter 4: Pick a Script to Write

_____

_____

_____

_____

_____

_____

_____

_____

_____

_____

_____

_____

_____

_____

_____

_____

_____

_____

_____

_____

_____

_____

Notes:
Chapter 5: Collect Your Five Laundry Lists

_____

_____

_____

_____

_____

_____

_____

_____

_____

_____

_____

_____

_____

_____

_____

_____

_____

_____

_____

_____

_____

_____

_____

_____

_____

Notes:
Chapter 6: Identify Your Sales Model

Notes:
Chapter 7: Outline Your Script

Notes:
Chapter 8: Write Your Script Section by Section

_____

_____

_____

_____

_____

_____

_____

_____

_____

_____

_____

_____

_____

_____

_____

_____

_____

_____

_____

_____

_____

_____

_____

_____

_____

_____

Notes:
Chapter 9: Persuasion Engineer Your Script

_____

_____

_____

_____

_____

_____

_____

_____

_____

_____

_____

_____

_____

_____

_____

_____

_____

_____

_____

_____

_____

_____

_____

_____

_____

_____

Notes:
Chapter 10: Revise, Improve, and Update Your Script

Notes:
Chapter 11: Types of Scripts

Notes:
Chapter 12: Swiping Successful Scripts

_____

_____

_____

_____

_____

_____

_____

_____

_____

_____

_____

_____

_____

_____

_____

_____

_____

_____

_____

_____

_____

_____

_____

Notes:
Chapter 13: Sample Scripts

Notes:
Chapter 14: Scripting GSA (Goals, Strategy, Action)

Notes:
Part III: Putting Scripting into Action

Notes:
Chapter 15: Getting Your Scripts Written

_____

_____

_____

_____

_____

_____

_____

_____

_____

_____

_____

_____

_____

_____

_____

_____

_____

_____

_____

_____

_____

_____

_____

_____

Notes:
Chapter 16: Rehearsal

Notes:
Chapter 17: Delivery

_____

_____

_____

_____

_____

_____

_____

_____

_____

_____

_____

_____

_____

_____

_____

_____

_____

_____

_____

_____

_____

_____

_____

_____

_____

_____

Notes:
Chapter 18: From Scripting to Spontaneity

Notes:
Bonus Chapter #1: 77 Sales Scripting Techniques

_____

_____

_____

_____

_____

_____

_____

_____

_____

_____

_____

_____

_____

_____

_____

_____

_____

_____

_____

_____

_____

_____

_____

_____

Notes:
Bonus Chapter #2: 10 Sample Probing Questions Scripts

_____

_____

_____

_____

_____

_____

_____

_____

_____

_____

_____

_____

_____

_____

_____

_____

_____

_____

_____

_____

_____

_____

_____

_____

_____

_____

Notes:
Bonus Chapter #3: 10 Sample Closing Scripts

_____

_____

_____

_____

_____

_____

_____

_____

_____

_____

_____

_____

_____

_____

_____

_____

_____

_____

_____

_____

_____

_____

_____

_____

_____

_____

Notes:
Bonus Chapter #4: Sample Referral Script

_____

_____

_____

_____

_____

_____

_____

_____

_____

_____

_____

_____

_____

_____

_____

_____

_____

_____

_____

_____

_____

_____

_____

_____

_____

_____

_____

Notes:
Bonus Chapter #5: 10 Sample Email Subject Line Scripts

Notes:
Bonus Chapter #6: Sample Conference Call Script

_____

_____

_____

_____

_____

_____

_____

_____

_____

_____

_____

_____

_____

_____

_____

_____

_____

_____

_____

_____

_____

_____

_____

_____

_____

_____

_____

_____

Notes:
Bonus Chapter #7: Sample Local Talk Script

_____

_____

_____

_____

_____

_____

_____

_____

_____

_____

_____

_____

_____

_____

_____

_____

_____

_____

_____

_____

_____

_____

_____

Notes:
Bonus Chapter #8: Sample Appointment Setting Script

_____

_____

_____

_____

_____

_____

_____

_____

_____

_____

_____

_____

_____

_____

_____

_____

_____

_____

_____

_____

_____

_____

_____

_____

Notes:
Bonus Chapter #9: Sample Scripts for Coaches

_____

_____

_____

_____

_____

_____

_____

_____

_____

_____

_____

_____

_____

_____

_____

_____

_____

_____

_____

_____

_____

_____

_____

Notes:
Bonus Chapter #10: Sample Phone Sales Script for Selling a Product or Service

_____

_____

_____

_____

_____

_____

_____

_____

_____

_____

_____

_____

_____

_____

_____

_____

_____

_____

_____

_____

_____

_____

_____

_____

Notes:
The 10 Best Ideas I'm Learning from This Book

(Extra lines included so you can add as you learn.)

_____

_____

_____

_____

_____

_____

_____

_____

_____

_____

_____

_____

_____

_____

_____

_____

_____

_____

_____

_____

_____

Glossary

Affirmation: A key word or phrase repeated to reinforce mindset.

Appointment booking: The act of scheduling a sales presentation meeting with a prospect. Distinct from lead generation and from delivering sales presentations.

Ask and be silent: A closing technique where you extend an offer and then remain silent while waiting for the prospect's response. Related to "hot potato."

Baseline: Your current sales performance numbers in areas such as leads, appointments, and sales generated over a specific time frame. Related to "track to run on."

Benefit of the benefit: An unstated or ulterior appeal associated with a stated benefit. (See "benefits.")

Benefits: Practical values of products or services. Distinct from "features."

Closing: The part of a sales presentation where you make the prospect a sales offer by offering them value in exchange for a price.

Database: A manual or automated system for managing contact information of prospects and clients.

Features: Descriptions of the components or specifications of products or services. Distinct from "benefits."

Follow-up: The part of the sales process where you resume contact with a prospect following the initial sales presentation.

Goal setting: A step-by-step procedure for systematically naming, prioritizing, and pursuing goals.

GSA (Goal Strategy Action): The three steps in putting a sales system into practical operation.

Hot potato: A closing or probing question technique where you put the burden of responding to a question or offer on the prospect until they reply, whereupon their reply returns the "hot potato" to you. Related to "ask and be silent."

Lead: A prospective customer.

Lead generation: The act of adding leads to your database by finding prospective customers, reaching them, and collecting their contact information.

Mindset: The habitual beliefs and attitudes that underlie your sales performance.

Objection handling: The part of a sales presentation after the close where you respond to prospect concerns about making a purchase.

Pre-client funnel: A technique for optimizing lead generation where you seek to funnel qualified prospects towards you while discouraging unqualified prospects.

Precession: The principle that action creates results and momentum that can have unexpected benefits, which would not occur if action were not being taken.

Prospect: A potential customer.

Prospecting: The part of the sales process where you seek to add leads to your database and establish contact with them.

Rapport: The act of establishing and nurturing a positive relationship of trust with your prospect. Underlies all other steps in the sales process.

Sales scripting: Writing and rehearsing sales presentations for optimal sequencing, wording, and delivery.

Sales Mountain: The step-by-step process for generating leads, booking appointments, and delivering sales presentations taught by Eric Lofholm.

Time management: A step-by-step procedure for systematically scheduling activities to meet priorities while saving time and energy.

Touches: The number of pre-sales contacts you make with leads in your database.

Track to run on: The number of leads, appointments, and sales you need to make to reach your sales targets. Related to "baseline."

Upsell: A sales strategy for selling related products and services to customers who have already bought from you.

80/20 rule (Pareto principle): A time management principle which advises spending 80 percent of your time on the 20 percent of activities responsible for generating the bulk of your business results.

For Further Reading

Abraham, Jay. *Getting Everything You Can Out of All You've Got: 21 Ways You Can Out-Think, Out-Perform, and Out-Earn the Competition*. New York: St. Martin's Press, 2000.

Aspley, John Cameron. *Aspley on Sales: A Guide to Selling in the Modern Market*. Chicago: Dartnell Corporation, 1967.

Belch, George E. and Michael A. *Advertising and Promotion: An Integrated Marketing Communications Perspective*. New York: McGraw-Hill/Irwin, 2011.

Bettger, Frank. *How I Multiplied My Income and Happiness in Selling*. New York: Prentice Hall Press, 1982.

Bettger, Frank. *How I Raised Myself from Failure to Success in Selling*. New York: Prentice Hall Press, 1986 (1947).

Burg, Bob. *Endless Referrals*. Third edition. New York: McGraw-Hill, 2005 (1994).

Butler, Ralph Starr, Herbert F. De Bower, and John G. Jones. *Marketing Methods and Salesmanship*. New York: Alexander Hamilton Institute, 1914.

Carnegie, Dale. *How to Win Friends & Influence People*. New York: Simon & Schuster, 1981 (1936).

Cialdini, Robert B., Ph.D. *Influence: The Psychology of Persuasion*. New York: Collins, 2007.

Feldman, Ben. *Creative Selling: The World's Greatest Life Insurance Salesman Answers Your Questions*. New York: Farnsworth Publishing Company, 1974.

Fenton, Richard and Andrea Waltz. *Go for No! Yes is the Destination, No is How You Get There*. Orlando: Courage Crafters, 2010.

Gamble, Teri and Michael. *Sales Scripts That Sell!* New York: AMACOM, 1992.

Gay III, Ben F. *The Closers*. Placerville: Hampton Books, 1987.

Gay III, Ben F. *The Closers: Part II*. Placerville: Hampton Books, 2000.

Getty, J. Paul. *How to Be Rich*. Chicago: Playboy Press, 1965.

Girard, Joe. With Stanley H. Brown. *How to Sell Anything to Anybody*. New York: Warner Books, 1977.

Gittomer, Jeffrey. *The Sales Bible: The Ultimate Sales Resource*. New edition. New York: HarperBusiness, 2008 (New York: William Morrow, 1994).

Good, Bill. *Prospecting Your Way to Sales Success: How to Find New Business by Phone, Fax, Internet and Other New Media*. New York: Scribner, 1997 (1986).

Hall, Roland S. *The Handbook of Sales Management: A Review of Modern Sales Practice and Management*. New York: McGraw-Hill, 1924.

Hickerson, J.M. *How I Made the Sale That Did the Most for Me: Sixty Great Sales Stories Told by Sixty Great Salesmen*. New York: Prentice Hall, 1951.

Hogan, Kevin. *The Psychology of Persuasion: How to Persuade Others to Your Way of Thinking*. Gretna: Pelican Publishing Company, 1996.

Holmes, Chet. *The Ultimate Sales Machine: Turbocharge Your Business with Relentless Focus on 12 Key Strategies*. New York: Penguin Group, 2007.

Hopkins, Tom. *How to Master the Art of Selling*. Introduction by J. Douglas Edwards. Fully updated and revised. New York: Business Plus, 2005 (first edition 1980).

Hoyt, Charles Wilson. *Scientific Sales Management: A Practical Application of the Principles of Scientific Management to Selling*. New Haven: George B. Woolson & Company, 1913.

Klaff, Oren. *Pitch Anything: An Innovative Method for Presenting, Persuading, and Winning the Deal*. New York: McGraw-Hill, 2011.

Kroc, Ray. With Robert Anderson. *Grinding It Out: The Making of McDonald's*. Chicago: Contemporary Books, 1977.

Kuesel, Harry K. *Kuesel on Closing Sales*. New York: Prentice Hall, 1979.

Kuesel, Harry N. *How to Sell Against Tough Competition*. New York: Prentice Hall, 1958.

Miller, Robert B. and Stephen E. Heiman. With Tad Tuleja. *The New Strategic Selling: The Unique Sales System Proven Successful by America's Best Companies.* Revised and updated with a new preface by Robert B. Miller. New York: Business Plus, 2005 (1998; first edition New York: Warner Books, 1985).

Moine, Donald, Ph.D. and Kenneth Lloyd, Ph.D. *Ultimate Selling Power: How to Create and Enjoy a Multimillion Dollar Sales Career.* Franklin Lakes: Career Press, 2002.

Moine, Donald, Ph.D. and Kenneth Lloyd, Ph.D. *Unlimited Selling Power: How to Master Hypnotic Selling Skills.* Englewood Cliffs: Prentice Hall, 1990.

Parinello, Anthony. *Selling to VITO: The Very Important Top Officer.* Third edition. Avon: Adams Media Corporation, 2010 (1994).

Person, H.S. (editor). *Scientific Management in American Industry.* New York: Harper & Brothers, 1929.

Pickens, James W. *The One Minute Closer: Time-Tested, No-Fail Strategies for Clinching Every Sale.* New York: Business Plus, 2008.

Popeil, Ron. With Jefferson Graham. *The Salesman of the Century: Inventing Marketing, and Selling on TV: How I Did It and How You Can Too!* New York: Delacorte Press, 1995.

Port, Michael. *Book Yourself Solid: The Fastest, Easiest, and Most Reliable System for Getting More Clients Than You Can Handle Even if You Hate Marketing and Selling.* Foreword by Tim Sanders. Hoboken: Wiley, 2006.

Rackham, Neil. *SPIN Selling.* Aldershot, England: Gower, 1995 (first published in 1987 as *Making Major Sales*).

Rackham, Neil. *The SPIN Selling Fieldbook: Practical Tools, Methods, Exercises, and Resources.* New York: McGraw-Hill, 1996.

Robbins, Anthony. *Awaken the Giant Within.* New York: Simon & Schuster, 1992.

Robbins, Anthony. *Unlimited Power: The New Science of Personal Achievement.* New York: Simon & Schuster, 1986.

Rosenstein, J.L. *The Scientific Selection of Salesmen.* New York: McGraw-Hill, 1944.

Sandler, David H. With John Hayes, Ph.D. *You Can't Teach a Kid to Ride a Bike at a Seminar: The Sandler Sales Institute's 7-Step System for Successful Selling.* New York: Dutton, 1995.

Schiffman, Stephan. *Power Sales Presentations: Complete Sales Dialogues for Each Critical Step of the Sale Cycle.* Holbrook, Massachussetts: Adams Media Corporation, 1993 (1989).

Scott, Walter Dill. *Aids in Selecting Salesmen.* Pittsburgh: Bureau of Salesmanship Research, Carnegie Institute of Technology, 1916.

Strong, Edward K. *The Psychology of Selling and Advertising.* New York: McGraw-Hill, 1925.

Strong, Edward K. *The Psychology of Selling Life Insurance.* New York: Harper & Brothers, 1922.

Thomson, Andrew H. With Lee Rosler. *The Feldman Method: The Words and Philosophy of the World's Greatest Insurance Salesman.* New York: Farnsworth Publishing Company, 1980.

Thompson, Willard Mead. *The Basics of Successful Salesmanship: A Self-Teaching Programmed Book.* New York: McGraw-Hill, 1968.

Tracy, Brian. *Advanced Selling Strategies: The Proven System of Sales Ideas, Methods, and Techniques Used by Top Salespeople Everywhere.* New York: Fireside, 1995.

Tracy, Brian. *The Psychology of Selling: How to Sell More, Easier and Faster than You Ever Thought Possible.* Nashville: Thomas Nelson, 2004.

Ziglar, Zig. *Zig Ziglar's Secrets of Closing the Sale.* Grand Rapids: Fleming H. Revell Company, 1984.

Ziglar, Zig. *Ziglar on Selling: The Ultimate Handbook for the Complete Sales Professional.* Nashville: Thomas Nelson, 2003 (1991).

Index

About Eric Lofholm

ERIC LOFHOLM is a master sales trainer who has helped over 10,000 students improve their sales results. Eric was not a natural born salesman, but was forced to learn sales fast when he found his first sales job on the line in 1993. Desperate after receiving a one-month probation warning from his supervisor, Eric turned to his mentor Dr. Donald Moine for help. Using Dr. Moine's system, Eric managed to make his monthly quota by just one sale and keep his job. By the end of the next month, he had quintupled his sales and become the top producer on his team. Soon, everyone wanted to know the secret of his success. Eric began sharing his sales secrets with his coworkers, and soon discovered he had a natural gift for teaching.

Eric honed his sales training skills as a trainer for Tony Robbins for three years from 1997 to 1999. He then founded his own sales training company, Eric Lofholm International. His clients have included Proforma, Blue Coast, Anthony Robbins Companies, and Laughlin Associates, among many others. Over the years, Eric has been responsible for helping his clients generate over $500 million in additional sales revenue. He has been able to teach his students how to duplicate his success, and has designed his sales training program so that the average sales representative can improve their results within thirty days. He offers affordable training both for corporate sales departments and for individual entrepreneurs who want to improve their sales skills.

Eric lives in Rocklin, California with his wife Heather and his four children Brandon, Sarah, Bella, and Emily.

For More Help

With Sales Script Writing

If you liked what you learned in this book and you'd like to learn more, your next step is to sign up for my virtual sales training opportunities. My four-level sales training system is designed to give you a "Black Belt in Influence," providing you with everything you need to progress from basic sales skills to becoming a master sales person yourself.

I offer live training events, but for your convenience, I also provide online sales training opportunities. You can learn directly from me from the comfort of your own computer or mobile device!

My virtual immersion events are normally $197 for three hours of intensive sales training, but because you bought this book, you can register yourself and a guest *free* by visiting this link and using this promotional code:

> **http://www.saleschampion.com**
> Promotional code: **system**

While you're on this link, you'll also get an opportunity to watch a free video series preview of what it's like to learn with me online. So visit the link, check out the videos, and sign yourself and a guest up for one of my virtual immersion training sessions. I look forward to seeing you there!

39500412R00183

Made in the USA
Middletown, DE
17 January 2017